AMERICA'S GAMBLE

AMERICA'S GAMBLE

PUBLIC SCHOOL FINANCE AND STATE LOTTERIES

Thomas H. Jones, Ed.D.
Professor of Education, The University of Connecticut
Storrs, Connecticut

John L. Amalfitano, Ph.D.
Chairperson, Special Education, Toll Gate High School
Warwick, Rhode Island

TECHNOMIC
PUBLISHING CO., INC.
LANCASTER · BASEL

America's Gamble: Public School Finance and State Lotteries
a **TECHNOMIC** ®publication

Published in the Western Hemisphere by
Technomic Publishing Company, Inc.
851 New Holland Avenue, Box 3535
Lancaster, Pennsylvania 17604 U.S.A.

Distributed in the Rest of the World by
Technomic Publishing AG
Missionsstrasse 44
CH-4055 Basel, Switzerland

Printed in the United States of America
10 9 8 7 6 5 4 3 2 1

Main entry under title:
   America's Gamble: Public School Finance and State Lotteries

A Technomic Publishing Company book
Bibliography: p. 175
Index: p. 187

Library of Congress Catalog Card No. 94-60030
ISBN No. 1-56676-092-5

To
Alison and Catharine

Each of us adds a little understanding.
And from all the facts assembled
there arises a certain grandeur.

(Aristotle)

CONTENTS

THIS book assesses the role of state lotteries in contemporary American culture. Viewed by some as a desirable tax instrument, by others as a recreational purchase, and by still others as a moral anathema, the lottery generates both social and political controversy. In order to counter the criticism, states have claimed that they are devoting lottery proceeds to worthy causes, especially the public schools.

Various opinions

Chapter 1 details reasons for the remarkable growth of state lotteries over the past thirty years. The role of federal and local governments in education finance has been declining, leaving the states with the major financial responsibility. States, however, must balance schools against other essential services, many of which have shown even sharper revenue growth. Lotteries are a sort of taxpayer surcease, helping to bridge the gap between limited funds and the states' inexorable revenue demands. Statistics in this chapter document the role of lotteries in state finances today. The discussion links lotteries with school reform movements for equalization, restructuring, and improvement.

Chapter 2 sets modern state lotteries in an historical context. Over the centuries, lotteries have had many uses, but they were *not* chiefly connected with education finance. Only in the eighteenth and early nineteenth centuries did lotteries begin to play a small role in school and college funding. Sponsors of earlier lotteries were private and the games sporadic. Then, as now, lotteries were the subject of moral debate. A prominent nineteenth century educational administrator, Presbyterian clergyman, and lottery entrepreneur serves as a foil for our own time.

In the contemporary period, lotteries have become permanent and wide spread, virtually an arm of government. Recent federal legislation clarifying a role for state lotteries is discussed.

Chapter 3 describes the operations of lotteries today. Since lottery policies vary somewhat from state to state, individual differences are discussed along with national trends. Much of the public policy literature on lotteries analyzes them as a state tax. Viewed in this way, the issues of lottery tax fairness become apparent. What types of people pay the lottery tax? How does the income, racial, social, and occupational status of lottery players compare with the average citizen? Questions of tax fairness and social efficiency are discussed.

Chapter 4 describes the model we use for lottery revenue analysis. Specifically, we are interested in whether or not lotteries influence public school finance in the fifty states and the District of Columbia. The few prior empirical investigations of this question have been oriented to one or two specific states. After reviewing those few prior studies, we developed a different approach that compares lottery states as a group with non-lottery states as a group.

Chapter 5 reports results of our group comparative analysis. In this study, four measures of support and effort for education were regressed on selected political, economic, social, and demographic variables. Interstate differences were statistically controlled. Findings address the following questions. What factors can account for differences among the states in their school financial support? What characteristics distinguish lottery states from non-lottery states? Do lotteries affect school spending? Does the claim that lottery revenues go exclusively for schools (versus other services) actually influence state fiscal behavior? Data are analyzed for the year 1987, one of the last years in which roughly half the states did have lotteries and half still did not.

Chapter 6 returns to the larger question of the role of lotteries in the contemporary American culture. Gambling is common to all times and places; individual gamblers have been the subject of many psychological investigations. Only in the modern time period, however, has lottery gambling been organized and supplied under the direct aegis of the state. The politics and sociology of state-operated gambling are topics which are not yet well developed.

The state makes the rules society must live by; the state also acts as entrepreneur and chief beneficiary of lottery games. We find these roles incompatible and suggest reforms which would directly impact states' claim that lotteries enhance public school finance.

ACKNOWLEDGEMENTS

WE want to express our thanks to the following individuals and organizations. Herbert Sheathelm and Richard Dempsey, professors at the University of Connecticut, read the manuscript carefully and provided insightful comments. Mark Shibles and Patrick Mullarney have given policy analysis expertise and support. Depa Roy, a member of the staff at the University of Connecticut library, initiated purchase of useful lottery materials. The University of Connecticut Research Foundation provided grant assistance for computing and travel. Donald Layton at SUNY, Albany, provided thoughtful advice and encouragement at various stages along the way. He also provided us with a very useful paper written by a former student, Vaughn Nevin. Staff of the Connecticut Special Revenue agency gave gladly their time and extensive bibliographic resources. Teri LaFleur, of *Gaming and Wagering Business,* provided significant documentation and unique information on the current status of lotteries available nowhere else. Carolyn Lindlau, Lisa McPherson, and Sharon Wilson read the manuscript and made useful editing suggestions. Susan Farmer and Dr. Joseph Eckenrode, of Technomic Publishing Company, Inc., gave the authors sufficient leeway to pursue this topic. The authors are responsible for any mistakes which remain.

INTRODUCTION

Revolutions are almost always the consequence of moral changes which have gradually passed on the mass of the community, and which ordinarily proceed far before their progress is indicated by any public measure. An intimate knowledge of the domestic history of nations is therefore absolutely necessary to the prognosis of political events.

Thomas Babington Macaulay

When the game goes on the market in April or May, Connecticut will be the first state in the nation to offer instant tickets for $25. "I'm after Nathan Detroit," said Susan White, the state lottery chief. "Detroit, the legendary high roller of the Broadway musical *Guys and Dolls,* would like the new game because the odds of winning are better than picking a winning horse at the track."

The Hartford Courant, December 17, 1992

WHEN the nineteenth century British historian Macaulay spoke of "silent revolutions," he had in mind those social changes that occur without much fanfare. They aren't imposed — they just happen. Contemporaries rarely appreciate their significance. Only in the next generation are they seen for what they are — massive changes that affect the daily lives of millions of ordinary people. Changes in computing, transportation, and communication are examples of silent revolutions in our own time.

In this book we argue that government-sponsored gambling may be a new silent revolution. Gambling itself is nothing new; but profound changes in technology and in the social structure may have changed its nature fundamentally. State governments have become chief sponsors of gambling to help support schools and other social services. Contemporary gambling legalizations are justified not so much on their own merits, but on the basis of the public revenue they will supposedly raise. In the public mind, this inevitably links educational support with the fortunes of the gambling industry—a controversial connection to say the least.

The silent revolution in gambling is supported by recent technological and social developments. Modern gambling depends on modern electronics. Records of each wager are kept instantly, inexpensively, and honestly. Gambling can now be managed by large national and international corporations without the crimes and financial scandals typical in the past. Wagers as low as one dollar can be very profitable. "Gaming" machines (the word gaming may now be used interchangeably with gambling) have bells, lights, and music. These are fun, and thus encourage more play.

Quite independent of developments in electronics, there has been a great expansion of government's role in society. In the past, people expected government to provide peace and order as the preconditions for economic prosperity. Now we expect government to provide social justice, not merely social order. We look to government to provide us with economic growth itself, not merely its preconditions. And we expect an ever growing array of social and educational services.

These aims have proven to be expensive. Government's share of the American economy has grown to about 34 percent, up from 26 percent a generation ago (Advisory Commission on Intergovernmental Relations, 1991). The public has become increasingly restive about tax increases even as government's social and economic agendas expand. We are caught in the bind of rising popular expectations and increased resistance to taxation.

Ostensibly at least, gambling loosens that bind. Since most forms of gambling have been outlawed in most areas of the country, any legalizations represent "new" tax money, an untapped source of government revenue. The gambling industry itself forms another major basis supporting legalizations. These factors, combined with increased leisure time, material prosperity, and changing moral values mean that more individuals want the opportunity to gamble. In order to engage in their favored activity, gamblers are quite willing to pay tax.

The silent revolution of gambling legalizations would be proceeding more rapidly but for lingering religious and moral compunctions. A significant minority of the population thinks all or most forms of gambling should remain outlawed. When policies are morally contentious, giving states the right to make their own legislation sometimes makes political sense; interstate variations mute the impact of any policy. But state control leaves a very uneven pattern of implementation across different jurisdictions, inviting competition and boundary crossing.

Ironically then, gambling policy in modern state governments must encompass *both* its potential for moral harm *and* people's desire to play. To deal with claims of moral harm, government taxes gambling heavily and imposes heavy regulations on gaming. This is supposed to discourage play. Heavy taxation also has the effect of adding to government coffers through a "voluntary" payment.

At the same time governments are discouraging gambling through heavy taxes and regulation, they have begun to accommodate gambling through an ever-increasing array of legal games. Accommodation takes the form of a sort of gambling continuum, from relatively "benign" games to addictive ones, and from private situations to commercial ones. Certain types of gambling are viewed as less harmful than others. The more benign gambling games (e.g., bingo, raffles) are legalized first and legalized more widely. The allegedly more addictive forms (e.g., casinos) are legalized later and less widely. Social play—at charities, churches, in private homes, etc.—has been more widely accepted than public games run by large commercial enterprises. But this is changing as the states take control.

In the last thirty years, fed by the trends mentioned above, America's appetite for gaming has grown enormously. Legalizations of all types of games have become more common across America. The continuum of legalizations has moved from relatively benign games and from clubs, church halls, and other private settings to the more addictive games held in public and commercial settings. By the 1990s, more Americans had more access to more forms of legal gambling than ever before. The games they play and the settings in which these games are held are more likely to be safe, legal, and honest (within the confines of the rules) than they ever were in the past. Access to commercial, legal gambling is increasingly close to home.

Large enterprises are best suited to meeting state governments' interests for provision and control. Compared to private and charitable games, public games can be taxed more easily. This helps meet government's inexorable and growing revenue needs. If games are public, more people are likely to play. The tax base is bigger. If revenue needs are satisfied more fully with public, commercial gambling, so is the need for fuller regulation. Larger, public corporations can work in concert with government. Such enterprises have absolutely no incentive to break any laws or steal any money. The legalized games are far too profitable. Larger firms can also exploit fully the new electronic gambling technologies, which require large initial capital outlays.

State-operated lottery games, the fastest growing form of American gambling in recent decades, are the focus of this book. From their beginnings on the East Coast in the 1960s, the games have spread to all corners of the nation. This multi-billion dollar industry and the players who support it have been the focus of considerable interest and research in the past two decades. More is known about lotteries than about most other forms of gambling. Currently in America, lotteries seem to be taking on a new significance, as they open the door to legalization of additional types of gaming.

Lotteries have some elements in common with other gambling games. Like slot machines, lottery terminals depend on modern electronics. Electronics provide speed, honesty, and accurate record keeping at a very low cost per wager. Compared to, say, poker, lotteries afford a longer period of time between the wager and the outcome. Lottery players presumably have a greater opportunity between bets to reconsider their financial position and decide whether to continue to play. For this reason they are considered to be one of the least addictive forms of gambling. Lotteries rely on no specialized knowledge in the way that, say, knowledge of the horses helps gamblers at the track. Nor do lotteries require the skills of the blackjack player. They are the purest form of luck. Lotteries are also one of the least social and least time consuming of gambling games. Among all games, they are the surest way to lose your wager. And perhaps for all these reasons, lotteries afford the dedicated gambler less pleasure than most other games.

A miscreant might say that lotteries are more socially accepted than other gambling games *because* they provide less pleasure. But whatever the reason, lotteries do not suffer from quite the level of moral opprobrium that more addictive gambling games do. The fact that lotteries are less addictive than many other gambling games is perhaps pleasing to many moralists. But this virtue is a defect from the viewpoint of the state. In its role as lottery entrepreneur, the state must encourage play.

Therefore, a second feature accounting for the acceptance of lottery games is the "good works" they support. The more taxes government has, the more good works it can do. This feature encourages not only lottery legalizations, but also ticket sales.

In state after state the cause of education finance has been invoked in connection with implementing or expanding lottery games. Schools, more than any other service, are the good work to be supported by this gambling tax. Allegedly, certain school services could not be provided through any other means. According to this line of thinking, any harm that gambling might do is balanced on the social scale by the good works it finances.

An investigation of this claim is central to the book. Does gambling promote good works, especially the enhancement of school funding? If lottery funds do fulfill this claim, then there really is a balance that must be weighed on a social scale. But if lotteries do not provide enhanced revenue levels, the claim of good works would be a false claim. State governments would be implementing their gambling policies under a false pretense, and this silent revolution might become a little noisier.

CHAPTER 1

State Lotteries for School Finance: The Controversial Connection

STATE lotteries generate billions of dollars for public use and private profit. Lotteries also generate a storm of controversy. On the one hand, the claim is made that state lotteries are detrimental economic, social, and political policy. On the other hand, lotteries are seen as a benign or at least harmless pastime and a painless way to finance needed government services.

The nation's public schools lie in the eye of this lottery storm. To establish and maintain support for the games, advocates emphasize lottery contributions to worthy causes, especially public education. And lottery advocates have been very successful. Three decades ago there were no state lotteries. By 1991 the federal government's fiscal crises, tax revolt measures, educational finance reform, and other factors had prompted thirty-six American jurisdictions to institute them as a supplemental means of finance.

New lotteries are being proposed for those states still without them, but even when games are adopted the controversies are by no means over. In those states which have had lotteries for years, education is invoked to justify new types of lotteries, including video, television, and sports betting. Going still further, some state and local governments have legalized casino gambling to finance relentless demands for more public services. All this has meant that the public's perceptions about educational finance and the overall condition of the school system are now inevitably linked to the lottery. Like it or not, school leaders and education policy makers are drawn unavoidably to the issues it raises.

This book is written around two broad questions. The first is this.

1

Does a lottery, or specific forms of a lottery, actually enhance school funding? That is, does the presence or absence of a lottery in a particular state affect the amount of money that state spends for public education? This is an empirical question, one on which new evidence is presented here.

A second line of questioning is broader. What stance should educators and educational policy makers take towards lotteries? This breaks down into subsidiary questions. Are lotteries a stable or growing revenue source? Are lotteries an acceptable method of raising money for schools and other public purposes? How does the existence of the games impact upon the state and the nature of society as a whole?

Broad questions such as these always lead to legitimate differences of opinion and policy conflict. The questions themselves, however, are by no means unique to our place and time. Lottery games have been prevalent throughout much of human history. In America, lotteries were held from the founding of the Jamestown colony in 1607 until their prohibition in 1894. Nor is the invocation of education to justify lotteries a new idea. Lottery funds were used to help establish some of the nation's leading universities—Harvard, Brown, and the University of Pennsylvania, among others. Despite attempts to justify them by worthy causes, however, lotteries have always been vigorously attacked by moralists and social reformers. They still are today.

Using insights from a variety of social science disciplines, this book discusses the broader questions that lotteries raise and evaluates the diversity of opinion regarding their nature and utility. Previously unpublished data are used to describe and analyze the relationship between state lotteries and financial support for education. Lotteries are examined from an aggregate, national perspective.

This fifty-state perspective is important. Here we do not address questions of whether a lottery in a particular state has targeted enhanced revenues to schools in a particular year. We look across all states, those with lotteries and those without them, to determine whether the presence or absence of lotteries has had any generalized effects on levels of school support throughout the nation.

Such an approach is justified by the lotteries themselves. Though the politics of lottery adoption, expansion, and rejection are specific to each state legislature, lotteries themselves are truly national in scope. The types of games are the same across states. The corporations involved in ticket production, sales, and promotion are national firms, and the demographic profile of lottery players is quite uniform throughout the country. The broader issues lotteries raise—moral, psychological, social, political, and economic—emerge again and again in every state's debate.

SCHOOLS AND THE STATE REVENUE CRISIS

The school revenue crisis in the states has been evolving slowly for three decades. At least three causes can be assigned.

(1) Chronic federal budget deficits slowed the rate of increase in federal aid to schools and other social services.

(2) A movement swept the country calling for equalized spending among local schools. The result was reduced reliance on the local school property tax—the principal cause of the spending variations.

(3) People became appalled at the schools' low academic standards. Educators called for "school restructuring," and, of course, still more money. "Equity and excellence" became the catch phrase.

All these reforms had to be financed by the states. But there was no more money.

Decline of the Federal Role

One place to begin the examination of these points is the huge increase in federal aid to the states in the 1970s. Initiated by the Nixon administration, intergovernmental aid in increasing amounts encouraged the states to tackle some of the intractable problems raised by the Johnson administration's "war on poverty." The problem with the war on poverty, some argued, was that it involved too much bureaucracy and control from Washington. Nixon's new initiative, called "revenue sharing," was supposed to eliminate a host of regulatory tangles. In broad terms, federal revenue sharing can be defined as aid with no strings attached. The rationale behind it is that states and localities understand their own problems better than the federal government does. Given the proper autonomy, they will solve these problems faster and more efficiently than the Washington bureaucrats.

Both the Nixon and the Carter presidencies favored the revenue sharing principle, though for different reasons. For Nixon, revenue sharing was a key domestic program. The hope was to empower state governments or, differently interpreted, to disperse the powerful anti-poverty lobbies that had concentrated in Washington during the 1960s. Under a decentralized system, they would have to turn to the fifty state capitals. During the Carter years, the recently established federal funding formulas and high inflation pushed revenue sharing to new heights.

During the 1970s, revenues of all governments grew by a colossal 300 percent. Growth in federal aid to states and localities was substantial, and steady. Grants quadrupled during the 1970s from $23 billion to $94 billion. By the end of that decade, states and their localities got one dollar from the federal government for every three that the states themselves raised in taxes (see Table 1.1).

In inflation-adjusted dollars, the state-local share of personal income rose only 16 percent. Still, by 1980 states were spending nearly one dollar in five that Americans earned. In other words, states increasingly spent money that they did not raise in taxes. States were to be the level of government providing new and expanded programs in health and welfare, and other social services. Revenue sharing heightened those expectations.

By the 1980s, trends in government spending and revenue sharing had slowed or reversed. Federal aid to states and localities, which grew 400 percent in the 1970s, grew by only 33 percent in the 1980s. Rates

Table 1.1. Trends in Governmental Revenue, 1969 to 1989.

Revenues by Government Level (in millions of dollars)				
			Intergovernmental	
Total			Federal to State-Local	State to Local
Year	Federal	State	Local	
1969	$ 205,562	$ 88,939	$ 89,082	$ 23,257	$ 26,920
1980	660,759	310,828	287,834	94,609	89,017
1989	1,092,660	586,687	532,013	125,824	157,652

Sources: *Governmental Finances in 1969–70; Governmental Finances in 1980–81;* and *Government Finance: 1988–89.* Washington, DC: U.S. Department of Commerce, Bureau of the Census, pp. 20–21; pp. 17, 30; and p. 2.

of increase in all forms and types of federal aid were drastically reduced, though the dollars continued to grow in absolute terms. By 1990, state and local governments got only about one dollar in every ten from the federal government. Yet the earlier spending seemed to have only heightened the need for more. New sources of state revenue had to be found (MacManus, 1990).

The School Finance Equalization Movement

Though the Reagan administration began a small program in the 1980s, most revenue sharing was not expressly intended for schools. In fact, federal school aid did not quite keep up with other forms of inter-governmental federal grants during the decade of the 1970s. Though federal aid to education grew from $6 to $22 billion, schools were something of a "poor relation" in relative terms.

School spending pressures emerged from quite a different source, the judiciary. The *Serrano* decision in California, *Robinson* in New Jersey, and related litigation across the nation demanded equilization of school spending across school districts within particular states. Judicial pressures for equalization continue with little abatement to this day (Kozol, 1991).

The problem identified by the courts has been the historically determinative concern for American school finance. With some specific exceptions, most states have always given school districts a basic grant to which local funds are added. This means that school spending decisions are made ultimately by some 16,000 localities. Wide variations in interdistrict spending result; it is not uncommon for some school districts to spend twice or even three times as much per pupil as other nearby districts spend. Thus the cost and types of educational services for all children are related to where they live. And, of course, children do not vote on the quality and finance of the educational services they receive. Based on arguments such as these, courts in state after state declared school funding arrangements to be unjust.

In one sense the courts' findings were nothing new. Local spending differences had been known for years, and intergovernmental grants had been used to reduce the spending inequalities. State revenues were rising slowly over time anyway, and the local share was decreasing. But the judicial decisions added new urgency to these long-term trends. To address court mandates, state aid had to grow in ever-increasing amounts.

Though the word "equalization" was interpreted variously by the courts, in practice it always meant reduced reliance on local finance. Localities have only one main source of revenue available to them, the property tax. Though property taxes doubled in their absolute amounts during the 1970s, reliance on the tax went down in relative terms. When adjusted for changes in personal income, schools were not costing more in 1989 than they were in 1969 (see Table 1.2). But states were paying for much more of the total school bill.

The combination of revenue sharing and judicial mandates had a profound effect on American school finance. Not expressly intended for education, federal revenue sharing freed other state resources for schools. Due mainly to state aid, total school expenditures tripled. Revenue sharing enabled states to address equalization pressures from courts — not completely, but in a modest fashion (Hickrod et al., 1992).

By the early 1980s federal funds were drying up while the judicial pressures continued unabated. States' school costs grew not only in absolute terms but in relative terms too. As the decade wore on, ballooning deficits further removed the federal government from the state-local financial picture. Washington was providing states with less and less help until, by the end of the decade, state governments had to tax more and more just to stand still. Education's share of all state aid rose from 50 percent to 63 percent. But spending inequalities among school dis-

Table 1.2. Trends in School-Related Revenue and Expenditure Adjusted for Growth in Personal Income, 1969 to 1989.

Year	Total School Spending (in billions)	Spending per $1000 in Personal Income		
		All State-Local Expenditures[1]	State-Local School Expenditures[1]	Local Property Taxes[2]
1969	$ 37.5	$176	$50.21	$45.74
1980	100.5	187	46.48	34.66
1989	185.2	219	45.19	35.17

[1]Includes direct and intergovernmental expenditures.
[2]Includes property taxes for school and non-school uses.
Sources: *Governmental Finances in 1969–70; Governmental Finances in 1980–81;* and *Government Finance: 1988–89.* Washington, DC: U.S. Department of Commerce, Bureau of the Census, pp. 18, 50; pp. 16, 95; pp. 6, 101–103.

tricts remained at unacceptable levels (Kellerman and Wulf, 1991). In doing more, the states were falling further behind.

School Reform and Restructuring

Pressure on the states for more school spending came from yet a third source, the school reform and restructuring movement of the 1980s. Though the rate of federal funding increases had slowed markedly, successive presidents, Reagan and Bush, sharply criticized school efficiency and competence. The national spotlight was cast on elementary-secondary education to an unprecedented degree.

Political rhetoric emphasized international comparisons of pupil learning. These comparisons were interpreted to show that, when compared with youths abroad, American students performed poorly on standardized tests of academic achievement. In the next generation, it was argued, America may not have enough language and mathematics skills to compete effectively in the international economic marketplace. According to this line of thinking, the nation would lose its preeminent standard of living and its dominant role in the world.

At the policy level, a variety of options were proposed to combat this trend. Among the more popular were curricular change, teacher retraining, increased efforts for dropout prevention, parent choice of their child's school, merit pay, longer school days, a longer school year, and increased requirements for student promotion and graduation.

The one element of consensus was that the worst test scores occurred in schools located in the nation's poorest areas, mostly inner cities. At a minimum, restructuring would require a better and more extensive array of services there. This fact puts states in a new revenue bind – they have to fund school improvement without new federal or local help.

A prime example of all three trends above is "Chapter 1," the compensatory education program initiated in 1965 by the Johnson administration. This "pass through" federal aid program uses states as a conduit, targeting federal funds directly to schools in the nation's poorest areas. Though it predated the revenue sharing idea, compensatory education aid doubled in the 1970s. In the 1980s, despite the national rhetoric about school improvement focused on low achievers, compensatory education enjoyed an increase of only about 35 percent.

Some of the reforms associated with the school restructuring movement would be very expensive; some have minimal financial implications. Since virtually every state and school district has its own reform and restructuring plan, it can never be clear how expensive the overall implementation would be. By the beginning of the 1990s it seemed clear that budget deficits would limit the federal role. Court sanctions and political equity considerations would limit use of the local school property tax. Whatever was to be done in education to "keep America competitive" had to be done by the states.

ENTER THE LOTTERY

Recent decades, then, have witnessed a reduction in federal and local financial support occurring simultaneously with heightened expectations for school performance. For reasons of both "equity" and "excellence," states—not other levels of government—got the school bill. The point, however, is not to suggest that states had uniform fiscal conditions across the two decades. In fact, there were tremendous variations among them. These variations themselves proved to be a potent engine for lottery adoption and expansion.

One of the fundamental problems in governmental finance is that states, in a sense, compete with each other. Particularly high taxes for schools or any other purpose are likely to drive people and business out of that state. On the other hand, states that can keep taxes low attract business and industry. The fifty American states form one large economic community, a free trade zone where people, businesses, and financial capital can move elsewhere. Under these conditions, substantial deviations from national average tax rates can be counterproductive. High taxes drive out growth and prosperity.

Another problem has become particularly acute in the last three decades. At any one point in time, financial conditions across the fifty states were very uneven. Regional and sectional recessions of long duration, coupled with "taxpayer revolts," have resulted in periods of limited growth in receipts from existing taxes in some states. Meanwhile, at the same time, tax receipts in other states were booming. With oil price shocks, bubbles in real estate, agriculture, and finance, it sometimes seemed as if one state's problems were another state's windfall.

Regional unevenness combined with the budget deficits to further reduce political demands for federal government assistance. Interstate competition in the nationwide free trade zone meant that it was difficult to raise traditional taxes. New revenue sources were sorely needed. But which revenue sources? Increasingly, state lotteries were seen to be part of the solution.

The Status of State Lotteries within the Gambling Industry

By 1990, lotteries were legal in thirty-four states and all Canadian provinces making them by far the largest and most ubiquitous form of state-run gambling enterprise (see Table 1.3). In terms of gross wager, Americans gamble about $21 billion per year on various forms of lottery games. This sum represents about one-half of 1 percent of personal income. About half the gross wager is returned in the form of winnings. Though casinos are by far the largest factor in the industry, lotteries are number two, having surpassed the pari-mutuel category in recent years. Pari-mutuels include horse racing, dog racing, jai alai, and associated offtrack betting parlors.

Card rooms include legal establishments open to the public for poker and other games. Indian reservations are increasingly offering full-fledged casino play on the Nevada and Atlantic City, New Jersey models.

But of all the major revenue producers, lotteries were the fastest growing form of gambling during the decade of the 1980s. The increase can be accounted for in two ways: the introduction of new games, especially lotto; and the addition of new states to the list of those sponsoring

Table 1.3. Trends in the Gross Annual Wager in the United States, 1982 and 1990 (in billions of dollars).

Year	1982	1990	Average Annual Percent Change
Casinos	$101	$226	10.6
Lotteries	4	21	22.7
Pari-mutuels	14	18	2.8
Charitable Games	1.2	4.5	17.8
Bingo	3	3.9	3.2
Legal Bookmaking	.5	2.2	19
Totals (includes games not listed)	125	286	10.82

Source: *Gaming and Wagering Business,* July 15 to August 14, 1991, Table 3, 12(7):40–41.

the games. States sponsoring lotteries grew by about one-third during the 1980s while lottery receipts grew by nearly 23 percent annually. Since gambling as a whole grew "only" by about 11 percent, per year, lotteries were the star performer. For purposes of comparison, personal income grew only about 6 percent annually during the decade. People were using larger shares of their income to place wagers.

The Status of Lotteries within State Government Finance

As Table 1.3 shows, in terms of gross wager casinos are about ten times as important a factor as lotteries. The picture changes dramatically, however, when the gambling scene is examined from the viewpoint of state governments. Until very recently, casinos operated in only two states, Nevada and New Jersey. More important, casinos return the majority of winnings to the players. Lotteries don't. In fact, only about half the lottery wager is returned to ticket buyers, for a phenomenal 50 percent "take out" (tax) rate.

In 1987 general sales taxes comprised 32 percent of states' revenues. Individual and corporate income taxes raised another 39 percent of the total. Much of the remaining share came from selective sales taxes called excise taxes.

This latter tax category is a potpourri, one sorely in need of attention and reform. There is only one guiding principle — political acceptability. Included among excises are items which are necessary to modern life, such as motor fuels and insurance, and items which are not, such as tobacco. Presumably it is inequitable to tax necessities at especially high rates. But states continue to do so.

Is the lottery truly an excise tax? Economists and public finance specialists are not unanimous on this point. Consumer spending for lottery tickets is entirely discretionary. But at the same time alcohol, cigarettes, and most other little luxuries are produced, marketed, and (in most states) sold at retail by private businesses. In the case of lotteries, the states control all phases of the operation. For this reason some observers consider lotteries not a tax but simply a source of revenue from a state business enterprise. Regardless of the nomenclature, lottery revenues do have a fiscal significance to the states (see Figure 1.1).

Much of the data for the empirical sections of this study apply to the year 1987, one of the last years in which there was still a sizeable

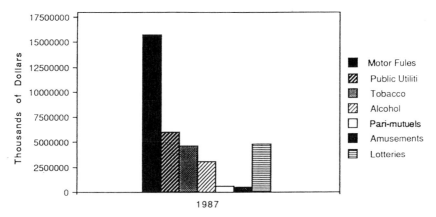

Figure 1.1 *State excise tax receipts (source: U.S. Department of Commerce, Bureau of the Census. 1988.* State Government Tax Collections, 1987. *Washington, DC: U.S. Government Printing Office, p. 4).*

number of both lottery and non-lottery states. In that year lotteries generated about $4.8 billion for the states, about 8.2 percent of all their excise tax revenues. Lotteries now rank in the mid-level among all state excises. They are smaller revenue producers than utilities and motor fuels, for example, but more significant than the taxes on other products such as tobacco and alcohol, which have moral stigmas attached. The fiscal significance of lotteries is due in part to the high rates at which they are taxed. Liquor and tobacco sell more product in dollar terms, but their sales are taxed at roughly half the rate of lottery tickets, making lotteries the states' leading revenue producer in the "sin tax" category (Karcher, 1989) (see Figure 1.2).

Despite the phenomenal growth of lotteries it is unlikely that they can ever account for a substantial share of state budgets. The tax base is simply too small when compared with the revenue-raising capacity of sales, income, and property taxes. Nevertheless, the heavy tax rate makes them attractive to states. More significantly, lotteries are viewed as a "voluntary" tax.

International Aspects

Lottery games of some description are played in most parts of the world. The single major exception has been the Moslem nations which are reluctant to adopt them for religious reasons. Lotteries know no politics: socialist Sweden and communist China hold lotteries. Probably the world's most lottery-crazed nation is Spain, home of the world's richest lottery, *El Gordo*—the fat one. Spaniards wager about 11 percent of personal income on all forms of gambling combined. The comparable figure in the United States is about 6 percent (Anon., "Gamble and Be Taxed," 1988).

Despite the ubiquity of the games, lottery information is scanty and subject to varying interpretation. Clotfelter and Cook estimate that about 100 "countries and territories" have legal lotteries (Clotfelter and Cook, 1989). The magazine, *Gaming and Wagering Business,* an authoritative source of information for the gaming industry, indicates that lotteries can be found in fifty-seven countries (Anon., "Lotteries Abroad," 1991).

Part of the discrepancy is undoubtedly explained by lack of standard definitions. For example, Canada has a national lottery *and* all its provinces hold lotteries. The sparsely populated prairie provinces have, from time to time, combined to hold multiple province games. At one time Ontario towns obtained separate licenses for their own lotteries. Under these conditions, how many lotteries *does* Canada hold?

Similar variability exists around the world, helping to explain vastly different counts. Government data collection efforts usually attempt to

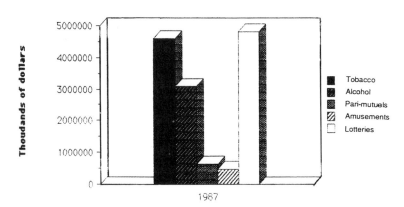

Figure 1.2 *States' receipts from "sin taxes," 1987 (source: U.S. Department of Commerce, Bureau of the Census. 1988.* State Government Tax Collections, 1987. *Washington, DC: U.S. Government Printing Office, p. 4).*

standardize and clarify definitions; but data on gambling is not yet a routine part of the U.S. government data collection efforts.

A second source of discrepancy may be explained by different definitions of the word "lottery." One conceptual distinction usually drawn between lotteries and other forms of gambling is the element of skill. Lotteries are games of pure chance. Poker and blackjack exemplify games involving an element of skill. Pure chance games historically have been associated with "passivity" because the player can't do anything to effect a win. Skill games are "active" games. They engage the players in an activity.

Modern electronics seem to be making the traditional distinctions obsolete. Video lottery terminals are active in that they have bells and lights; they are operated directly by the player. Yet VLTs have a lottery-iike aspect because skill cannot affect the outcome.

The Distinction between Gambling and Investment

The difference between gambling and investment is not simply one's likelihood of making money. Gambling redistributes money among those making wagers. Business investments, on the other hand, are undertaken to create new wealth and capital. Profits, stock dividends, and bond interest are the compensation paid to investors for the *risk inherent in a business situation*—the risk of business failure. Lotteries and other forms of gambling *create risk where none previously existed* for the express purpose of rewarding the sponsor.

Some people find that this distinction has moral overtones. Natural risks must be undertaken for the purpose of building civilization. Extra and unnecessary risks should be avoided. Persons accepting this distinction view business profits as being qualitatively different from gambling. Others seem unimpressed by this distinction. Explaining why he didn't buy lottery tickets, one stock market adviser quipped on T.V., "I never gamble off the job."

The distinction between gambling and investment can blur at the margins. In the 1950s the British government sold numbered savings bonds which had an unusually low interest rate for that time. In exchange for the lower interest rate each numbered bond became part of a lottery pool. All bond holders got a rate of interest, albeit a low one. If your bond number was drawn you got a large tax-free prize. In light of the discussion above, this financial instrument may be considered part investment and part gamble. Pure speculation in options and futures contracts may be considered another form of gambling.

Revenue Earmarking and Its Effect on School Spending: The Issue of Fungibility

In an effort to secure legalization of state lotteries, advocates stress public service needs. Lotteries are allegedly a revenue source without any pain, a voluntary way to meet expenses for schools, health care, or anything else, without raising taxes. A frequently used tactic is to dedicate or *earmark* lottery revenues directly for one or more popular public services.

This earmarking concept is crucial, and controversial. It is crucial because some of the political support for lotteries derives in part from its applicability. Lottery proponents claim that earmarking revenues for noble causes promotes lottery ticket sales and mitigates any dubious moral consequences resulting from state-sponsored gambling. Earmarking is controversial because opponents claim that it has no substantial effect. According to this line of thinking, all that lotteries do is to substitute lottery funds for other funds. In the grand scheme, state aid to local schools or other services may not be enhanced at all.

In this context lottery opponents raise another financial concept, the *fungibility* of money. Fungibility simply means that one thing can be substituted for another thing of a like kind. In the present context, fungibility means that states might reduce their school appropriations from non-lottery sources and use earmarked lottery revenues instead. Technically, the state statute would not be violated. But practically this would simply be a ploy, confusing the average citizen. There is, then, a controversy over efficacy and the viability of earmarking (Gold, 1990).

Do states' lottery arrangements really affect how much school revenue they raise? On this matter state statutes, at least, are quite clear. By 1987 twenty-two states and the District of Columbia sponsored lotteries. Eleven jurisdictions assigned the revenue to the general fund for allocation at the discretion of the state legislature, or used the funds for revenue sharing to cities and towns. Five states allocated lottery profits for public projects, such as transportation, conservation, economic development, and senior citizens programs. The remaining seven states earmarked all or major portions of their lottery revenues for primary and secondary education. The specific earmarking policies of each state are noted in Chapter 5.

The Educational Significance of the Earmarking Question

The earmarking of lottery revenues has, or potentially could have, a major financial impact on education. To illustrate, consider federal aid to schools. Federal school aid is widely acknowledged to have been a major force in service for target populations—the poor, the disabled, bilingual groups, and so on (Odden, 1991). In some situations, lottery revenues exceed these well-known and widely studied federal programs. By 1987, states' lottery revenues earmarked for schools equaled nearly one-third of total federal school aid. Michigan, Ohio, and New Jersey are among those states that designate lottery profits for public education. In those three cases the lottery revenues actually exceeded their federal school aid.

States' profits from lotteries continue to grow. By the early 1990s this form of gaming was generating $10 billion per year. There can be no question, then, that lotteries conceivably might help education finance. Some claim they do already (Celis, 1991; Ellis, 1990).

Most educators and finance specialists, however, find that lotteries do not actually add to school support; they insist that the public is misled on this point (Allen, 1991). The question is whether lotteries in actuality have the economic and social characteristics which make them desirable as a public revenue instrument.

Much of the argument centers around the concepts of tax earmarking and the fungibility of state revenues. These are topics to which we return throughout this book.

Moral and Social Judgments about Earmarking

Lottery initiatives have triumphed through voter referenda, constitutional amendment, and legislative enactment. Despite such political success and popular acceptance, the question of whether a state should authorize a lottery raises a host of moral issues.

The claim of earmarking tends to reduce political opposition in two ways. First, it proposes added financial support for popular public services such as education. Secondly, it neutralizes claims that the games have pernicious social, economic, and moral ramifications (Tifft, 1984; Clotfelter and Cook, 1987; Frey, 1984; Mikesell and Zorn, 1986; Suits, 1977, 1979). Proponents emphasize projected lottery contributions to the attainment of worthy causes such as education (Blakey, 1979; McCann, 1987; Weinstein and Deitch, 1974). Ticket buyers can do good for others while possibly doing well for themselves.

It is well established that linking lottery revenues to education creates political support for lottery legislation (Batch, 1987; Ezell, 1960; Hancock, 1987; Sirkin, 1985; Weinstein and Deitch, 1974). Historically this has also been true. Ezell (1960) notes that "some petitions for academy charters were merely preliminary to requests for lottery franchises." Focusing on this age-old political maneuver, he adds,

> A corollary to the feeling that "the end justifies the means" is the American, perhaps universal, interpretation that taint can be taken off peccant money by devoting part of the proceeds to "good" causes.

This theory is embraced by lottery advocates today and is echoed by Batch (1987) in the *Handbook of U.S. Lottery Fundamentals*. He advises, "It may be prudent from a political and practical approach, to attract the support of special interest groups. . . . This overture may aid in the passage of the legislation." In the final analysis, the moral and financial questions are inextricable. The empirical and economic claims blend together with the social and philosophical.

Along opposite lines are claims that lotteries are actually counterproductive to school finance, that they see as more of an obstacle than an enhancement. Thomas and Webb (1984) contend that using lotteries to finance education "may be more of a political ploy than an actual benefit." Bill Honig, California's former Superintendent of Public Instruction, maintains that schools in his state would have been better off without the lottery. He warns, "People think we're sitting on a pile of dough when we're not. But that perception has made it easy for the state to make what otherwise would have been politically difficult cuts in the education budget" (Shapiro, 1988). Educators fear that lotteries may supplant rather than supplement educational funds; others argue that the fundamental right of education should be dependent upon revenue sources which are more solid and stable (Anon., "Are Lotteries Really . . .," 1987; Hallberg, 1987; Hartwig, 1987; Stewart, 1987).

Adversaries charge further that lottery earmarking for schools leads taxpayers to the dangerous misconception that education finance crises are, to a large degree, alleviated by this "voluntary tax" (Byard, 1987; Hallberg, 1987; Sample, 1987; Snider, 1987). For example, in California, lottery advertisements have ended with the phrase, "Our Schools Win, Too." Intense outcry from educators was responsible for the removal of TV promotions which depicted a smiling teacher strolling through a classroom full of computers (Von Drehle, 1987).

From its initial operation in January 1988 to September 1988, the Florida lottery collected $359 million for public schools (Shapiro, 1988). But some critics in Florida assail lottery promoters with warnings that lottery profits will be offset by cuts from what normally would be allocated from other taxes. A 1986 strike by Oakland, California, teachers was ended with a salary hike funded by proceeds from the state lottery (Shapiro, 1988).

Assertions by both proponents and opponents are often partially substantiated. But the lack of any large-scale research makes it difficult to substantiate any claims about the efficacy of earmarking, pro or con. Commenting on this scarcity of empirical data, Pipho (1987) asserts, "Lotteries are not going to go away . . . we badly need better research data on the impact they have on educational funding."

CONCLUSION

Recent events have propelled states' school spending upwards. State judicial systems have been demanding educational finance equalization. The historic role of the local property tax in elementary-secondary education finance has been reduced. America's students are considered poor performers on standardized tests of academic achievement, leading the national economy into decline. International economic competition has heightened interest in school reform. Improvement programs, particularly for the inner cities, heighten the need for state revenues. At the same time, federal budget constraints dictated a diminution of the national role. For these reasons the states' share of school costs has risen.

Though many reasons could be cited for lottery adoption and expansion, the most important is the growing financial crisis in the states. Taxes at all levels of government have grown substantially in the last twenty years, straining traditional revenue sources. This fact and allegations of government inefficiency and immorality have led to tax revolts. States are caught in a storm of pressures to reduce taxes while providing more services. Lotteries are one result. By 1991, thirty-six American jurisdictions had implemented lotteries—with education, more than any other state function, mentioned as the object of the new revenues. Demands for education continue to play a key role in decisions to expand the games—e.g., video lotteries, sports lotteries. At the same time, some political leaders call for new forms of gambling on riverboats and in land-based casinos. Proposals to expand gambling to new locales are now seriously considered.

Before commenting on these possibilities, it is necessary to take a step backwards, to examine the history of lotteries in America. Only if we understand this broad foundation will we be able to understand future potential, and future danger.

CHAPTER 2

At the Margins of History and Morality

NEARLY every society has used some form of decision making based on chance. In this very broad sense, lotteries are as old as human history. But lotteries have not always been associated with money, or with the sponsorship of worthy causes. These aspects of the game have evolved over recent centuries.

This chapter provides an overview of the lottery's development from ancient times to the present. Emphasis is placed on the social issues which surrounded the games in times past, and which continue to our own day.

THE BIBLICAL CASTING OF LOTS

A primary distinction exists between lotteries as "games" and the much older practice of "casting lots." Lot casting, known among the ancient Hebrews, Arabs, Chinese, Teutons, and other premodern cultures, is very possibly as old as civilization itself. The modern games, however, may be thought to have their origins in the Italian Renaissance of the fifteenth or very early sixteenth centuries. The key distinction is the expectation of profit.

"The lot is cast into the lap; but the whole disposing thereof is of the Lord." This quotation from Proverbs (16:33) sums up much of the ancient world's view of lotteries. In the Biblical context, lots were cast for one purpose only: to reveal God's will. They were used only in difficult and urgent matters, and only in those cases where human powers of reasoning were inadequate to the task at hand. Thus, lot casting was always a last resort activity and not associated with play for money or prizes. Lots revealed God's will in issues such as the determination of a guilty party (Joshua 7:13) or selection of a king (1 Samuel 10:20–21). Other ancient societies had much the same view; for some the casting of lots was a serious matter. The ancient Greeks, for example, used this same method for the selection of certain important office holders.

This ancient usage has modern analogues. A coin toss may be used to avoid conflict, reach a speedy decision, or break off an argument. No one loses face; nor is there moral significance to winning a coin toss. In modern times, however, the coin toss has normally been relegated to fairly insignificant decisions. It has been considered, however, as a means of deciding organ transplants (Karcher, 1989).

To the ancient mind, casting lots and gambling were completely different activities. They had nothing to do with one another. It remains, then, to say a word about Judeo-Christian attitudes toward gambling, since to our modern minds, lotteries and other forms of gambling converge (Devereux, 1980; Brenner and Brenner, 1990).

The Bible contains no express prohibitions against gambling. However, scholars consider this not so much an omission as a sign that the matter was well settled in Jewish law. From its inception, Christians frowned on the practice. The Roman patriarch Tertullian wrote, "If you say you are a Christian when you are a dice player, you say what you are not, for you are a partner with the world." Gambling thus entails implicit faith in luck, chance, or fate—something wholly different from Divine Providence.

Historic opposition to gambling derives not only from Judaism and Christianity, but also from the third great religion of the West: Islam. Islamic injunctions are as authoritative as those in Judaism and Christianity. The Koran warns the faithful that "there is great harm in both liquor and gambling and also some profit for people, but the harm is greater than the profit . . . so turn wholly away from these satanic devices" (2:220).

In our day, some people believe that as a form of gambling, lotteries are a sin against God (Wall, 1990). We tend to call such opinions "fundamentalist"; however, many religious people hold this view who are not necessarily fundamentalists in other respects.

Most contemporary religious denominations take a more permissive attitude. Religiously based opposition to gambling often centers on excesses, citing the immoral consequences that can result from the act, rather than on its intrinsic evil (Bell, 1976).

ROMAN AND EARLY EUROPEAN LOTTERIES

In the ancient world, lotteries had secular uses. For example, wealthy Roman households used lotteries as means of distributing door prizes to guests at parties. Only rarely and sporadically were they used as a supplementary means of public finance. The first modern European games with monetary prizes were organized in Florence in 1530 (Brenner and Brenner, 1990). Before that date, merchants in medieval Europe had used them as a source of profit; they sold their finest and most expensive goods by lottery, finding that method more profitable than outright sale. The Venetian government recognized the revenue potential of these games and established a very profitable monopoly in lotteries (Ezell, 1960).

Later, lotteries played an important role in the French government's fiscal structure. The games were especially popular among subjects who had been burdened with enormous taxes to support the profligate spending of monarchs. Though refusing to pay increasing taxes, the people demonstrated a great willingness to participate in lotteries.

EARLY ENGLISH AND COLONIAL LOTTERIES

Beginning in 1569, England granted royal sanctions to lottery games designed for public and private fund raising. During the subsequent 250 years, lotteries played a role in the economic and social history of that county (Ashton, 1898). In the 1600s, the Virginia Company of London operated lotteries to finance the settlement of Jamestown.

In 1606, King James I of England chartered two private companies for the purposes of settling and exploiting the New World (The Virginia Company of London and the Virgina Company of Plymouth). The Plymouth Company was inactive for over a decade, but in 1608 the first settlers of the London Company arrived at their destination in the wilderness. The settlement proved not to be a source of easy riches, however. The situation was quite the opposite. By 1611, the company was foundering. Instead of producing the hoped-for profits, the settlement,

appropriately named Jamestown, continuously drained company resources.

Having no clear prospects of a profit, merchant-owners petitioned
the king for financial relief. In 1612 the company was granted rights to
conduct "one or more" lotteries, probably only the third such license
ever to have been granted by an English sovereign (Ezell, 1960). The
company immediately set to work. Advertising circulars were posted
conspicuously throughout the leading towns of the realm. Promoters
solicited endorsements from leading citizens and offered assurances of
honesty. The *Pepys Ballads* record what surely must be the first ever
advertising campaign for "American" lotteries. The following doggerel
was sung to a popular tune of the day.

> *London, live thou famous long,*
> *thou bearest a galant minde:*
> *Plenty, peace and pleasures store,*
> *in thee we daily find.*
> *The merchants of Virginia now*
> *hath nobly took in hand,*
> *The bravest golden Lottery,*
> *that ere was in this land.*
>
> *A gallant house well furnished foorth,*
> *with gold and silver plate.*
> *There stands prepared with prizes now,*
> *set foorth in greatest state.*
> *To London worthy Gentlemen,*
> *goe venture there your chance:*
> *Good luck stands now in readiness,*
> *your fortunes to advance.*
>
> *It is to plant a kingdom sure,*
> *where savadge people dwell:*
> *God will favour Christians still,*
> *and like the purpose well.*
> *Take courage then thou willingnesse,*
> *let hands and hearts agree:*
> *A braver enterprise than this,*
> *I thinke can never be.*

(Rollins, 1929)

For the first time in American history—but by no means the last—a lottery offering was linked to the hope of personal financial gain and support of an important public purpose.

The logistics of lottery management in the seventeenth century were quite unlike those of today. Tickets were printed in advance with no certainty of their subsequent sale. Weeks, months, or even years might elapse between any single individual's purchase of a ticket and prize drawings. Since prizes were established without prior knowledge of the ultimate ticket sales, there was some risk to the entrepreneurs. Ticket purchasers had no advance knowledge of the odds or, in many cases, even the date of the drawing. If no date was specified, potential buyers might well postpone their purchase. But if everyone postponed, the prize drawing would never be held—the classic catch-22. Under these conditions it is not surprising that lottery promoters often specified a date for the award of prizes, then announced postponements owing to poor sales.

The first Virginia lottery, however, might be considered an ideal model for its day. Ticket sales extended over only six weeks. The drawing was conducted on the appointed day and was considered to have been fairly conducted (not all of them were). The winner of the gold and silver plate mentioned above was not a "gentleman" as implied by the *Ballad,* but he was as solid member of the middle class, one Thomas Sharplisse, a tailor.

The only problem was ticket sales. The first Virginia lottery made money for the company. But many tickets remained unsold, pointing to a chronic problem among early lotteries. Tickets tended to be overpriced, and those of the Virginia Company lotteries were no exception to this general rule.

There are several reasons for overpricing. Seventeenth century businessmen, lottery organizers included, had only the dimmest perception of the relationship between the price of a product and the demand for that product. It seemed prudent from the lottery organizer's point of view to charge the highest ticket price which could plausibly produce maximum revenues. If a ticket could be sold for £1 instead of one penny, why not ask the larger amount? High-priced tickets save time, printing, and marketing costs.

Secondly, the poorer classes had little access to currency or specie. Much payment in the seventeenth century was "in kind." Employers provided food, clothing, and shelter in exchange for labor of the lower classes, but little cash. Lottery tickets, of course, had to be purchased with cash. And thirdly, lottery success depended on advertising, some of which was in print. Many poor people could not read. Sales efforts were focused on those who seemed most able to buy. "Gentlemen" were the only class of people with access to knowledge about lotteries and substantial sums of money to spare.

Owing to the poor sales of the first Virginia lottery, the second ticket offering made substantial steps to broaden the market. The "little standing lottery" lowered the ticket price to twelve pence — still a substantial sum by standards of the time. New marketing strategies were employed. The Privy Council, an official arm of government, was prevailed upon to urge London guilds to buy tickets (en masse) as a patriotic gesture (tailors' and grocers' companies each bought £50 worth). A new prize structure was developed, assuring that big investors would receive at least a token prize. And prize winners could take payment in the form of shares of Virginia Company stock, offered at a discount to the market price.

Despite these enticements, the second or "little" lottery was only a limited success. Though tickets were first offered in 1613, the drawing was not held until 1615, implying that sales were — to put the best possible light on it — slow. The little lottery was the Virginia Company's last lottery in London. Henceforth, the company moved its base of lottery operations to England's provincial cities.

The provinces, of course, contained in the aggregate many more people than the capital did. The profit potential was very large indeed. But ticket sales outside London were harder to manage. Furthermore, the company was quite naturally composed of seamen, merchants, and traders. Lotteries were a new and essentially sideline business. For these reasons, the company followed a management pattern that was to become typical of lotteries right through to the nineteenth century: they hired independent agents to conduct their ticket sales.

Under this type of arrangement, the company became a ticket wholesaler. Agents (independent entrepreneurs) bought tickets from the Virginia Company at a discount and sold them at a higher, retail price. This solved the problem of offering tickets across far-flung distances, but it created a series of new problems.

Agents had fewer incentives for honesty than the direct government licensee. Since most of them were small businessmen who did not take a long-term view, agents realized that they could make vast sums from the manipulation of ticket sales in a single lottery. When agent misbehavior or crime was discovered, moral opprobrium was likely to be directed at first, the principal, and only later at his agents. A scandal or shift in the political winds might cause the principal to lose his lottery license; but the principal's recovery of funds from an agent depended on proof in court.

One problem was negotiated commissions and ticket discounting. Agents subcontracted ticket sales to "runners." High ticket prices meant that many people bought part of a ticket; but only the seller had any knowledge of the odds. Under these conditions, it was impossible to know exactly how many full-price billets were actually sold, and how many were controlled by the agent or his friends. Simply keeping track of tickets passing through many hands was a complex and time-consuming task. In the local lotteries of the Virginia Company, calculation of profits and compensation structures were matters of continuous discussion between agents and the principal.

Less scrupulous agents had many possibilities open to them. One was to attempt manipulation of prize drawings. To guard against this, the Virginia Company, and sponsors of American lotteries later on, attempted to enlist the support of substantial and well-respected local citizens in each community. They might attend drawings or even conduct them. This type of connection also proved to be a good marketing technique. Another tack was to enlist children, appointed by the dignitary, to pull winners. This worked particularly well when billets were drawn from huge drums; the children could climb right inside. Under such conditions it was quite easy to hide the winning ticket "up your sleeve," one origin of the modern metaphor.

Lottery promoters also had "dream books" containing lists of lucky numbers. Claiming prior successes, writers' advice might be based on apparitions, associations with important events, and, of course, dreams themselves. Advice might be contingent upon dates, ages, birth months, etc.—creating their own complexity and need for interpretation. Dream books were a popular source of "wisdom" and an added source of sales and revenue.

Another dubious practice was called "insurance": essentially the purchase of a portion of a whole ticket. This practice was associated with another early marketing modification, the running lottery. The running lottery was developed to address the problem associated with the time lapses between ticket sales and prize drawings. As we have seen in the case of the second Virginia lottery, these lapses could be two years or more in some cases. Unsold tickets meant that the prize drawing must be postponed; but if the postponements were expected, everyone would wait to buy. In the extreme case the drawing would never be held, and the later history of lotteries records such instances.

The running lottery circumvented this problem by rewarding early buyers with more chances to win. Daily or weekly drawings would award smaller prizes, with the grand or "capital" prize saved until total ticket sales reached acceptable levels. Insurance was a bet that a particular number would be drawn on a particular day within a longer running lottery. Since insurance was good for one day only, it was cheap.

This was its particular virtue from the seller's viewpoint. Insurance opened an entirely new and lucrative market, namely, poor people who could not afford the price of a ticket. With little risk, an agent could run a profitable sideline business in insurance. Some unscrupulous agents sold insurance on unsold tickets, yielding a truly risk-free profit! It seems likely that insurance yielded far greater profits than straight sales under the old agency system.

The extent of these abuses is not recorded in connection with the Virginia Company's local lotteries in England's provincial cities. On the other hand, the practice of selling insurance was not expressly forbidden by laws of the day. Records of lotteries conducted in the next century are replete with documentation of the practice; and, judging by compaints against the Virginia Company, it seems at least possible that it was not unknown as early as the seventeenth century.

Thoughts of truly mass participation were still far from the minds of these early entrepreneurs of the Virginia Company. It was not until the nineteenth century that lottery promoters began to recognize and fully exploit the purchasing power of the poorer classes. By that time, the poor were beginning to be reimbursed for their labor with currency or specie. The money economy grew, and lotteries were one use to which money could be put. Lotteries are sometimes given credit for the spread of investment banking and the accumulation of large sums of financial capital. They enabled the "wealth of the little fellow to be tapped for financial investment" (Ezell, 1960).

English colonists transported the lottery to America. Economic and political dependency on England, and the economic necessities of an underdeveloped, barter economy with limited specie, rapidly paved the way for the lottery in the New World. In America, the lottery financed numerous public projects, including education.

RELIGIOUS AND MORAL VIEWS TAKE
A MODERN FORM

There has always been a certain degree of religiously based opposition to gambling. Pious anti-gambling activists have tended to view fortune as a golden calf—a false god potentially crowding out faith in the true God. But despite their passion, in the increasingly secular societies of the seventeenth, eighteenth, and nineteenth centuries it is probable that religion could not, by itself, quash gambling.

Side by side with these religious objections, there arose a more rational, secular set of arguments against gambling. In place of scripture, these arguments tended to stress the negative psychological, economic, and sociological effects of gambling. Though never completely absent from older writings, pragmatic arguments have a particular appeal to the modern mind. According to this line of thinking, the very activity of gambling leads to loss of property, laziness, preoccupations, and impetuous behavior. Similarly, gambling fosters the idea of attaining "something for nothing." Reward without effort is an aspect of gambling particularly inimical to the Protestant ethic (Devereux, 1980). Moral arguments may or may not be religiously based. But religious and secular reasoning, though based on different premises, frequently produce the same political and moral stance.

There are moral and religious arguments *for* gambling, as well as against it. Oddly enough, one of the early justifications for moderate gambling came from a seventeenth century Puritan clergyman, one Thomas Gataker. In *The Nature and Use of Lots,* Gataker deals with both religious and secular objections. On the religious side, Gataker argues, God doesn't micro-manage every little event. God could intervene to determine winners and losers, but doesn't; therefore, gambling results should not be taken as a Divine signal. Gataker's response to the secular argument that gambling has evil consequences is to counsel moderation. The size of the wager should be such that losing will not harm one's living standard. The prize should be such that winning would not constitute a vast windfall. Gataker poses another—perhaps the major—argument in support of gambling. For many it is a pleasurable way to socialize, an intrinsically enjoyable activity (Brenner and Brenner, 1990).

A CASE IN POINT: ELIPHALET NOTT

Eliphalet Nott serves as an exemplar of many of the political, moral, and administrative issues already raised. His career serves as a bridge to our own time and to our central topic. Nott was an inveterate tinkerer, inventer, and lottery entrepreneur, as well as an ordained clergyman with strong moral compunctions, the president of a college, and the superintendent of the New York State Literature Lottery. This remarkable man of many talents worked and dreamed of a system of education supported, in good part, by means of lotteries.

By the standards of his time, Nott's dream was by no means outrageous. As early as the colonial period, King's College (later Columbia University) had benefitted from lotteries. During the Revolution, lotteries helped to finance the war, and enabled government to undertake other public works. In 1805 the New York legislature authorized the state's first lottery for education. Half the proceeds went to academies and half went to the public schools.

In 1804 Nott took over the fledgling Union College in Schenectady, NY. Starting as an unpaid lottery lobbyist in nearby Albany, he deftly wooed both the Federalist and the Republican factions in the legislature, arranging compromises suitable both to aristocratic Columbia University and to the upstart democratic colleges such as Hamilton and his own Union.

For his efforts Nott was awarded the superintendency of New York's Literature Lottery. A list of the recipients of the 1814 lottery gives a flavor of the coalition-building which must have taken place. Hamilton College received $40,000, Union College received $100,000, and other, smaller endowments existed for Asbury African Church and its school, various medical colleges, and the New York State Historical Society. Nott arranged for the state legislature to give Columbia University the land on which Rockefeller Center is now situated as a side payment, in lieu of participation in this particular lottery (for Columbia, this proved to be a very wise choice).

In addition to superintending lotteries and running a college, Nott was a leading Presbyterian clergyman. He saw nothing inconsistent in these roles. Nott's rationale for lotteries was twofold. On one hand were the good works lotteries enable "well-regulated seminaries [which] diffuse science, promote morals and perpetuate the liberties of a free state." On the other hand, lotteries in themselves were not seen as a bad thing. Nott's rationale carefully distinguished lotteries from the "sinful," more active games which used time unprofitably, misapplied property, and substituted wagering for expansion of the mind. Lottery ticket buyers, in his view, were not really ordinary gamblers. Instead, they were to be considered simply participants in the laws of nature. He wrote:

> The gambler challenges Natural Law. But the man who *hazards only* [italics supplied] invites the operation of natural law because, in hazarding, he consciously serves God's purpose. If the hazard serves some principle of public policy, if the transaction will, on the whole, be beneficial to the parties or the community, no crime is committed. (Hilsop, 1971)

In Nott's mind, lotteries were a neutral event for individuals — redistributive, but neither particularly helpful nor harmful. It was the social result which justified lotteries to Nott. Nott implicitly followed Gataker's line of thinking — up to a point. As did Gataker, Nott distinguished between the gambler who defies natural law by risking a large sum, and the "hazarder" who risks only a small sum. But Nott goes beyond Gataker, justifying the lottery by its publicly beneficial results.

For Gataker, moderate gambling is an entirely personal affair, acceptable to the Lord if it doesn't get out of bounds. For Nott, the lottery could be justified on both a social and personal level. The state sponsor wanted lotteries for worthy causes; the individual wanted lotteries because they were an inexpensive way to have a good time. The entertainment factor was important, for were charity the main purpose, the ticket buyer could always make a direct donation instead. Nott's is, of course, the dominant contemporary viewpoint. It is the joining of this dubious personal want with finance of social goods which makes lotteries acceptable to present-day Americans. If either one of the two justifications were missing, we would not have lotteries in their present form.

Nott's "dual justification" theory seems unfounded in a Biblical context. For the ancient Hebrews, casting of lots had an overriding social goal: learning God's will in predicaments impossible to address through human knowledge alone. For Nott, the social goal is already abundantly clear and made known to the public at every drawing. The Literature Lottery, for example, provided salutary funding for schools, colleges, a poor black church, etc. We are not learning God's will by gambling. In buying lottery tickets we are *doing* God's will, which we already know.

Nott claimed to reconcile his lottery with injunctions from the ancient Biblical world, but this was not always as successful as he might have wished. It is hard to find a religious sanction in a political act of the New York legislature. Many of his contemporaries viewed Nott's rationale for the modern money games as entirely non-Biblical, and consequently, he was the target of scathing criticism.

Nott would not have argued that any and all actions are justified simply because they produce a good result. He simply weighed the sale of lottery tickets against the social benefit of building a college, and concluded that a little "hazarding" now and then was quite all right. He drew the line at games such as poker and roulette, where the "hazarder" could all too easily become the "gambler."

Then, as now, the moral arguments were not particularly determinative of public policy. Ultimately Nott was relieved of his superintendency, not because of any philosophical or moral misgivings, but because of administrative considerations. There were scandals and mismanagement of funds, similar in many ways to the problems with the English nearly two centuries earlier. Nott was not above using funds for certain dubious purposes of his own, and he himself became the subject of official investigations. Periodic economic downturns and collapses resulted in thousands of unsold tickets, and delayed drawings and prizes. Ultimately, these scandals redounded to the detriment of the superintendent. Reviled by these events and by growing public criticism, New York implemented a constitutional prohibition against new lotteries in 1820. That state's lotteries eventually wound down, but not until President Nott had raised a handsome sum for his beloved Union College.

Though he was perhaps the most adventuresome of the early lottery educator-entrepreneurs, Nott was hardly unique. Lotteries were a widely accepted revenue-raising device, advocated by many educators during the eighteenth and early nineteenth centuries. Lottery tales of the 1820s have a distinctly modern ring. But in state after state, the growth of lotteries was accompanied by financial scandal. As time wore on, these financial abuses made lotteries increasingly controversial.

THE LOUISIANA LOTTERY

Frequent cases of fraud and default helped extinguish enthusiasm for and interest in lotteries. Criticism from newspapers, churches, labor and farm organizations, and other reformers led to the gradual erosion of these "money raffles." By 1862 most states had either enacted anti-lottery legislation or banned the games in their state constitutions. With a reputation for being corrupt and fraudulent, by 1878 Louisiana was the only state in the union where lotteries maintained a toe-hold.

In 1868, a New York gambling syndicate received authorization from the Louisiana legislature to institute the infamous Louisiana Lottery. The legislature granted the enterprise monopolistic control and prohibited the sale of all other lottery tickets in that jurisdiction. The company agreed to make annual payments of $40,000 to the state for twenty-five years. The Louisiana Lottery continued its nationwide operation through postal and interstate commerce facilities; it penetrated all states. To insure government tolerance of this profitable operation, the company bribed legislators and manipulated elections (Weinstein and Deitch, 1974). It lobbied in Washington in an effort to forestall the passage and enforcement of anti-lottery laws. To enhance the activity with an element of honesty and respectability, former Confederate generals sometimes conducted the drawings. As sales and profits soared, the Louisiana Lottery Company paid dividends of 170 percent in 1889 (Sullivan, 1972).

The Louisiana Lottery stirred national criticism with the way it flagrantly disregarded the anti-lottery statutes of other states. Moreover, anti-lottery statutes were ineffective in preventing citizens in other states from participating in the Louisiana games. Between 1878 and 1890, anti-lottery bills were introduced in every session of Congress. Finally, in 1890, federal postal regulations banned the mailing of all lottery-related materials (Weinstein and Deitch, 1974).

In 1892, the Louisiana Lottery Company offered the state an annual payment of $1,250,000 for the right to continue its activities. Whether or not to accept the offer was a major issue in the state's gubernatorial election of 1892. When the electorate defeated a state lottery amendment, the legislature banned ticket sales.

The company then attempted to avoid postal regulation by moving its headquarters to Honduras and operating through an express company at Port Tampa, Florida. With intense pressure from anti-lottery groups, "the lottery was dealt a fatal blow by the passage of a bill prohibiting the importation of lottery material and the use of all forms of interstate commerce by lottery companies" (Weinstein and Deitch, 1974). With the enactment of federal statutes, the Louisiana Lottery, the last legal lottery until the adoption of the New Hampshire Sweepstakes in 1963, was put out of business. After playing an instrumental role in the early economic development of the United States, lotteries entered a period of abolition in America.

REEMERGENCE OF LOTTERIES IN
THE TWENTIETH CENTURY

By the mid-twentieth century, the Louisiana debacle was beyond the memory of most living Americans. During the depression, and again in World War II, the lottery idea was advocated in Congress and in several state legislatures (Ezell, 1960; Mueller, 1935; Weinstein and Deitch, 1974). Beginning in 1937, lottery bills were introduced on a regular basis in New Hampshire (Commission on the Review of the National Policy toward Gambling, 1976). That state had no broad-based sales or personal income taxes, so municipalities and schools were almost completely dependent upon onerous property taxes. In its perennial efforts to avoid the levy of traditional taxes, the New Hampshire legislature, after intense political struggle, resurrected the lottery to support public education.

Governor King and other proponents were undoubtedly aware that public acceptance could be enhanced by earmarking lottery proceeds for good causes. In his final argument to the legislature, King asserted,

> Constantly increasing demands for school facilities, at a time when our people are already carrying a cross of taxation unequaled in American history, make it our duty to initiate programs which will relieve this heavy burden on the people. (Weinstein and Deitch, 1974)

During the first few years, lottery revenues in New Hampshire fell far short of projections. High ticket prices, infrequent drawings, and federal restrictions on marketing were blamed for the poor performance (Hancock, 1987). In 1964, the first year of the New Hampshire Sweepstakes, net lottery revenues of $2.8 million generated approximately $24 per pupil. The money represented a significant percentage increase in state aid to schools, but did little to curtail burgeoning local property tax rates (Rosen and Norton, 1966).

Despite the questionable success of the New Hampshire Sweepstakes, proponents in other states, eager to capitalize on the lottery phenomenon, solicited support of special interest groups by including their causes as beneficiaries of the games. In 1967 and 1970, state lotteries were introduced in New York and New Jersey respectively. With marketing problems similar to those encountered in New Hampshire, the New York lottery failed to generate the revenue that had been predicted. But New Jersey, with profits of $30 million during the first six months, reaffirmed the revenue potential of this "voluntary tax" when it introduced a new, fast game, and a 45 percent payout rate. New York, New Hampshire, and many other states which followed, restructured their games to reflect the winning ingredients New Jersey had discovered.

These early state lotteries of the twentieth century were severely limited by federal restrictions that had been imposed in the 1890s. It was illegal to broadcast, use the mails, or transport tickets or lottery information across state lines. These constraints left government lotteries at a decided disadvantage when compared with the illegal competition. At times, some states either disregarded these restrictions or used methods to circumvent them.

In defiance of Justice Department action to enjoin the practice, the New Hampshire Sweepstakes Commission accepted "requests to participate in its sweepstakes from every state in the Union" (Commission on the Review of the National Policy toward Gambling, 1976). To circumvent the no-transport laws, New Hampshire issued duplicate ticket stubs to non-residents so that the original ticket never left the state. Winners could not claim their prizes directly with this receipt, but upon presentation of the duplicate stub they were issued the official ticket, which entitled them to collect their prizes.

New York also developed a device to evade federal laws against interstate transportation of lottery materials. Lottery officials would open a bank account for out-of-state winners. The account would be promptly closed and the bank, not the lottery commission, would mail a draft to the lucky non-resident (Bird, 1972). Prohibited by FCC regulations from broadcasting lottery promotions, the Michigan lottery placed ads on Canadian T.V. stations which could be received in parts of Michigan. Of course, in avoiding federal regulations, these states paid the cost of reduced efficiency.

In hearings conducted by the Commission on the Review of the National Policy toward Gambling (1976), state lottery directors argued that federal regulations violated states' rights to conduct their lawful businesses and to raise revenues as they deemed fit. They added that anti-lottery statutes had been enacted to protect the public against privately owned lotteries, rather than against lotteries operated by the states themselves. The commission agreed with this reasoning and recommended that the federal government exercise restraint by recognizing the rights of sovereign states to develop their own gambling and revenue-raising policies.

In 1974, Attorney General William Saxbe warned lottery states of his intent to take legal action against jurisdictions that were violating federal lottery statutes. Representative Peter Rodino of New Jersey, and Senator Philip Hart of Michigan, promptly introduced legislation exempting states from many of the federal restrictions (Commission on the Review of the National Policy toward Gambling, 1976).

Blakey (1979) assailed the conduct of lottery states with regard to federal restrictions. According to him, this sort of conduct had the long-range effect of compromising citizens' respect for the law. He writes,

> When convenient, they have obeyed the letter, though rarely the spirit, of the federal lottery laws. When compliance was too costly, they simply violated the law secure in the knowledge that the Justice Department could hardly treat states like common criminals. When federal officials finally tried to make states conform to the law, the states pressed Congress to make laws conform to the states . . . their extraordinary ability to find and to create loopholes in the federal criminal code does little to engender public respect for law. States that require lawful behavior from their citizens should ask no less of themselves.

The expansion of the thriving U.S. lottery industry over the past decades reflects the positive feelings and attitudes of Americans toward these revenue-producing activities. The volume of ticket sales is evidence of popular acceptance of the games. By the late 1980s, the annual per capita bet exceeded $100 in eight states. In Massachusetts, per capita sales topped $215 (LaFleur, 1988a).

Politicians and industry leaders recognize this popularity, and continue to introduce lottery bills in those jurisdictions where lottery prohibitions remain. For example, in Kentucky, Governor Wallace Wilkinson included the legalization of the lottery as part of his 1987 election platform. Citizens in that state approved a lottery referendum by a sixty-one to thirty-one margin in November 1988. In November 1986, the Florida lottery referendum received more votes than any candidate in the state (Morain, 1987). North Dakota is the only state to have defeated a lottery referendum since New Hampshire introduced the modern lottery in 1963. According to *Gaming and Wagering Business,* 58 percent of the North Dakota electorate turned down the lottery "largely out of fear that it might have diverted money from charities, the beneficiaries of that state's blackjack game" (Anon., "The Electorate of . . .," 1988).

Since the Great Depression, legislators in the United States Congress have periodically introduced bills to establish a national lottery. Franklin D. Roosevelt, noting the lottery's success in Ireland, favored a national lottery for charitable purposes (Ezell, 1960; Mueller, 1935; Weinstein and Deitch, 1974). Representative L. Cary Clemente of New York introduced legislation that would have used proceeds from a national lottery for veterans' benefits. In 1955, Congressman Paul A. Fino from New York, called his lottery bill "a simple, painless, and honorable way for the U.S. Government to earn at least $10,000,000,000 a year . . ." (Ezell, 1960). Introduced in 1983, H.R. 89 would have established a national lottery to help finance the Old Age, Survivors and Disability Insurance program (U.S. Senate, 1984). Obviously, efforts at the state level are far more successful.

CURRENT LEGAL STATUS: A ROLE FOR LOCAL SCHOOL LOTTERIES

To date Congress has not enacted a national lottery. It has, however, clarified the status of state lotteries, removing them from their legal twilight zone. The Charity Games Advertising Clarification Act of 1988 expressly permits advertising, listing of prizes, and other lottery information in the media of the state where the particular lottery is conducted, and in the media of adjoining states. The national newspaper, *USA Today,* publishes states' lottery drawings.

But other elements of lotteries still remain only partially clarified. Interstate and foreign ticket sales are still apparently prohibited. The national legislation now allows non-profit organizations and "commercial organizations" to conduct lotteries, subject to state laws, provided such lotteries are a "promotional activity" and "clearly occasional and ancillary to the business of that organization" (U.S. Congress, 1988).

The 1988 federal statute also appears to allow schools, school districts, and other local government agencies to operate lotteries. States would, however, have to enact enabling legislation expressly authorizing local government lotteries and setting the ground rules for their conduct (Jones, private communication). As of this writing, the authors are unaware of any local lottery legislation enacted or proposed in any state. The idea receives further treatment in the last chapter.

CONCLUSION

Since early modern times, lottery promoters have promised revenues to a wide variety of popular causes. Sponsorship of popular causes was intended to enhance revenue production. Yet revenue streams from lotteries were highly unpredictable. Throughout history lotteries have been a last resort funding mechanism. The games could meet only a small portion of their sponsors' financial needs, and rarely could major public or private works be undertaken consistently on the basis of ticket sales.

Lottery administration was an expensive and time-consuming task in relation to the revenue produced. Fraud, or at least the possibility of fraud, was inherent in the management of early lotteries. Lotteries might run for an undetermined number of months or years. The time between purchasing the ticket and the drawing of prizes, especially the capital prize, might be extended indefinitely. In some cases the drawing might never take place. Selection of winning billets was fraught with potential abuse.

For all these reasons, lotteries were considered a shady opperation. In the 1880s church groups, newspapers, and farm organizations were the most formidable lottery opponents. These moralists organized anti-lottery campaigns, claiming that lotteries capitalized on human frailities, exploited the poor, and compromised the work ethic. Arguably, however, it was the corruption in the games, not the moral opposition, which sealed their doom.

Despite their dubious qualities, however, lotteries were instrumental in the economic and social development of the United States. During the Revolutionary period, approximately 75 percent of all lotteries licensed in the colonies before 1776 were used for civic or colonial causes (Ezell, 1960). George Washington, Benjamin Franklin, Thomas Jefferson, and other colonial leaders, cognizant of the revenue potential of lotteries, promoted these games to fund projects such as schools, churches, bridges, roads, and the Revolutionary War effort itself.

In his classic work, *Fortune's Merry Wheel,* John Ezell (1960) asserts, "It would be difficult to overestimate the lottery's value in the development of the American educational system." From 1790 to the Civil War, approximately fifty colleges and 300 lower schools received revenues generated by lotteries. Harvard, Princeton, Brown, and Yale are among the institutions of higher learning which were financed in part by this public gaming. During the early part of the nineteenth century, lower schools and academies from Mississippi to Michigan to New York were reaping the benefits of legalized gambling. Between 1826 and 1844, Rhode Island alone generated a total of $200,000 for its general school fund.

As the games proliferated, their character changed profoundly. Direct sale operations were replaced by large-scale lotteries that promoted their tickets statewide and nationally. The games changed from a small-scale public revenue device to a large business enterprise. The private sector became more involved. Independent brokers bought tickets at wholesale prices from sponsors and resold them for profit. In some cases, private contractors operated the entire lottery and hired brokers to market tickets. According to Weinstein and Deitch (1974),

> The type of organization and promotion they developed laid the groundwork for techniques later used by other large-scale businesses beginning to emerge in the United States. The operations of these lottery enterprises also provided the framework for investment banking and stock brokerage firms. In essence, commercial lottery promoters were amalgamating small savings for capital investment purposes.

Despite Ezel's observation above, almost no general surveys of American history or American education pay lotteries much attention.

It is perhaps not surprising that educational historians (particularly those of an earlier day) may have overlooked this "seamy side" of the educational enterprise. Although the fate of the American nation has never quite hung on the spin of a lottery ball, the contribution of lotteries to American history certainly deserves more attention than it has so far received.

CHAPTER 3

Operational Characteristics of State Lotteries

AS state lotteries become more prevalent, the importance of examining them as an instrument of public revenue becomes more pronounced. The information presented in this book is designed primarily to describe the impact of lottery revenues on the provision of public education, but a fuller treatment of the topic warrants the consideration of broader issues related to this public policy area.

This chapter attempts to sort out the political, economic, and social dimensions of lottery policy. The games are discussed within the wider context of gambling in America. Emphasis is placed on those aspects of the games that are of current topical interest, including morality, legality, sponsorship, revenue production, and the dedication of proceeds to worthy causes. A description of contemporary lottery operations provides a background for understanding current research and viewpoints.

TYPES OF LOTTERY GAMES

The Commission on the Review of the National Policy toward Gambling (1976) defines a lottery as "a form of gaming in which chances to share in a distribution of prizes are sold." A lottery has three basic elements: a wager by the player, chance, and a prize. Although states differ in the types of lotteries they offer, the modern state lotteries have used five general types of games.

Table 3.1 shows what lottery games operated in each state in 1991. So

Table 3.1. Types of Lottery Games Operating in 1991, by State or Province.

State/Province	Instant	Lotto	Numbers	Passives	VLTs
United States					
Alabama					
Alaska	•				
Arizona	•	•			
Arkansas					
California	•	•	•	•	
Colorado	•	•		□	
Connecticut	•	•	•	□	
Delaware	•	•	•	□	
Florida	•	•	•		
Georgia					
Hawaii					
Idaho	•	★	•		
Illinois	•	•	•	□	□
Indiana	•	•	•		
Iowa	•	•			▲
Kansas	•	•			
Kentucky	•	•	•		
Louisiana	▲	▲			
Maine	•	•	•	□	
Maryland	•	•	•	□	
Massachusetts	•	•	•	□	
Michigan		•	•	•	
Minnesota					
Mississippi					
Missouri	•	•	•		
Montana	•	•			•
Nebraska					□
Nevada					
New Hampshire	•	•	•	□	
New Jersey	•	•	•	□	
New Mexico					
New York	•	•	•	□	
North Carolina					
North Dakota					
Ohio	•	•	•	•	
Oklahoma					
Oregon	•	•	•		▲
Pennsylvania	•	•	•	□	
Rhode Island	•	•	•	•	
South Carolina					
South Dakota	•	•			•

(continued)

Table 3.1. (continued).

State/Province	Instant	Lotto	Numbers	Passives	VLTs
Tennessee					
Texas					
Utah					
Vermont	•	•	•	□	
Virginia	•	•	•		
Washington	•	•	•		
Wash. DC	•	•	•		
West Virginia	•	•	•	□	•
Wisconsin	•	•			
Wyoming					
Puerto Rico		★	★	•	
Virgin Islands	▲			•	
CANADA					
Alberta	•	•	★	•	▲
British Columbia	•	•	•	•	
Manitoba	•	•	★	•	
New Brunswick	•	•	•	•	★
Newfoundland	•	•	•	•	★
Northwest Terrs.	•	•	•	•	
Nova Scotia	•	•		•	
Ontario	•	•	•	•	
Prince Edward Isl.	•	•	•	•	★
Quebec	•	•	•	•	
Saskatchewan	•	•	•	•	
Yukon Terr.	•	•	•	•	

•Legal and operative.
★Implemented since July 1990.
▲Authorized but not yet implemented.
□Permitted by law and previously operative.
Source: *Gaming and Wagering Business,* Vol. 12, No. 8, August 15–September 14, 1991, pp. 18–19.

called "passive games" constituted early lotteries of the 1960s and 1970s. These passives consisted of prenumbered tickets which were chosen in periodic drawings. This is the classic version of the lottery, now reserved mainly for the charity raffle (raffle is a euphemism preferred by charity game operators).

Instant games, introduced in Massachusetts, became very popular in the 1970s and soon overshadowed the earlier passive ones. With instants, players become more active as they purchase tickets, rub off a waxy substance, and learn instantly whether or not they have won. Instant lotteries have particular appeal to the impulse buyer who prefers immediate knowledge of the outcome (Hancock, 1987).

A third version, called the numbers, is fashioned after its illegal counterpart. In this game, players place bets on a three or four digit number which they select, and the wager is recorded on an on-line computer terminal. A winning number is usually chosen daily and broadcast over the media.

Lotto, a pari-mutuel game, is now widespread and the most lucrative of all the games. Lotto has many variations, but in one popular variant players select six out of thirty-six numbers. Odds of matching all six are less than one in a million. If a winning number is not selected, at least part of the jackpot is rolled over to the next drawing. Raising the pool of numbers to select from greatly reduces the chance of winning the jackpot. A slight change in the game can produce odds of 1:10,000,000 or even worse. However, long odds greatly raise the size of the potential jackpot.

Drawings are held weekly. As jackpots accumulate to millions of dollars, media coverage increases and ticket sales generally skyrocket. For example, immediately preceeding the drawing of a $67 million jackpot—the nation's largest lottery jackpot to that date—Illinois lotto machines were distributing 30,000 tickets per minute (Associated Press, 1989). Media interest in huge prizes such as these amounts to free advertising for states. Winner payoffs of tens of millions of dollars regularly become front-page national news.

A new form of play—video lottery terminal (VLT)—is legal in five states as of this writing (Anon., "Which States . . ., 1991). Terminals are located mainly in bars or other establishments that are off limits to children.

Inserting money into an electronic machine gives the player an automatic turn at play. Combinations of numbers are generated randomly. When the particular turn at play results in a winning number, there is a payoff. For losing numbers the machine keeps the money. The fact that VLTs are really nothing more than a form of slot machine is not lost on policymakers. Their legalization has been slowed due to the association of "one-arm bandits" with full-fledged casino-style gambling. As states' revenue needs grow inexorably, many industry observers feel that the VLT will become the fastest growing form of play in the remainder of the decade.

Opposition of professional organizations, notably the National Football League, has quashed attempts to initiate sports lotteries. Though widespread abroad, sports lotteries now seem somewhat less likely to become a major factor in the industry's future.

Still newer forms of lottery betting are in the planning stages. Their common threads are automation and a more active form of player engagement. Eliminating the need for store clerks or other direct sales staff would increase profits. Greater involvement on the part of buyers is intended to increase sales. Tickets might be dispensed through bank teller–like machines in convenient locations. They might be purchased over the phone, using touch tones to pick numbers. Or they might be dispensed as an enticement for other purchases. Airlines have considered including them along with frequent flyer miles.

A current, highly controversial proposal is the television lottery. Viewers at home might purchase tickets through interactive T.V. during a weekly or nightly lottery variety show. Televised drawings would be punctuated by singing, dancing, and other forms of entertainment, giving players time to place their bets electronically. The concept is being seriously discussed by leading corporations. It would be particularly suited to a national lottery, if one ever were to be enacted (Yoshihashi, 1991).

THE POLITICS OF STATE LOTTERY ADOPTION

In the past generation, state lottery adoption has grown apace. What theoretical or conceptual insights can explain this new development? For Elazar (1972) a dominant ethos or mentality pervades the electorate of each state, influencing political decision making across time. Elazar identifies three different sorts of political cultures—moralistic, individualistic, and traditionalistic. Moralistic states have high concerns for the welfare of the "have-nots." They can be expected to spend more on services like education and anti-poverty programs. Individualistic states have a greater concern for growth and development. They can be expected to adopt a tax structure and regulatory posture that is pro-business. Traditionalistic states are low on innovation. They emphasize continuity, one-party control, and, often, rule by a few leading families.

Interstate migrations of the population, the rolling recessions of the past twenty years, tax crises, more intensive media coverage, and other recent events may have rendered the permanency of these conceptions associated with any particular state somewhat obsolete. It may be more accurate to think of Elazar's characteristics dominating at particular times or with respect to particular issues (his own thinking did allow for hybrid states).

These explanations of state policy have to do with what might be termed the political uniqueness of various states. They assume that each state is largely independent of the rest. But is each state truly the independent agent Elazar hypothesized? Berry's (1987) study of lottery adoptions proposes two other models, "diffusion" and "hierarchy." The diffusion concept implys that states' tax policies will tend to follow those of closely neighboring states. Hierarchy emphasizes the role of a few leading states, larger and more powerful than the rest, which are trend setters. Empirical support for these models can be found in the work of Stover (1990).

The models are also persuasive intuitively (see Figure 3.1). Modern state lotteries began in New Hampshire, the quitessential individualistic state. (The motto on that state's license plate is "Live Free or

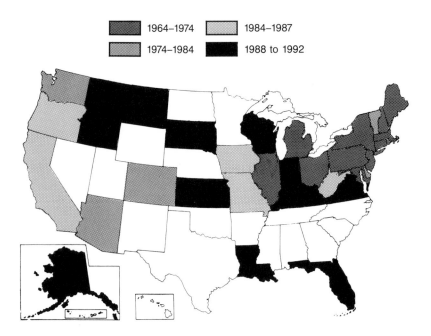

Figure 3.1 *Lottery states by first year of adoption.*

Die.") Some large densely populated "moralistic" states of the urban Northeast have education and welfare spending well above the national average. They adopted next. In the East, interstate travel is quick and routine. Other states may have initiated games because of the revenues they feared would be sacrificed to bordering states. This accords with the diffusion model. Lotteries then spread down the "hierarchy" to the Midwest and West, with the "traditionalistic" South and some of the smaller western states remaining as holdouts.

The concepts of hierarchy, diffusion, and state political culture are useful background variables for interpreting state policy. But they are not immediate causes for lottery adoption. It is economics which determines lottery politics. In every state the games are viewed as an alternative to new or increased taxes. Political, business, and sometimes education leaders promote them as a "painless" way to finance needed public services. Political theory may tell us which states are more ripe for lottery adoptions and expansions, but it takes a revenue gap to actually force the decision.

TECHNOLOGY

The success of modern state lotteries is due, in large part, to the reliability, technical sophistication, and high speed of modern data processing (Hancock, 1987). Distribution, sales, payments, and commissions are maintained by computers. These machines can verify purchase locations and serial numbers.

To date, computers also have made it virtually impossible to forge or steal tickets. Much of the chicanery associated with past lotteries appears to be impossible now—something that has doubtless contributed greatly to their current popularity. Computers have also contributed immensely to the economic viability of lotteries by making the necessary record keeping feasible at the cheap price of one dollar. The importance of these developments can hardly be overemphasized. Technology is *the* element in the modern games which distinguishes them from their predecessors.

Technical changes, in turn, portend changes in government administration and regulation of lotteries. Technology influences the revenue potential. In dealing with the newer forms of interactive lottery games policymakers are continually confronting an expanded set of legalization alternatives. This confrontation forces new decisions about how government will cater to the nation's gambling habit.

LOTTERY ADMINISTRATION

A state lottery commission establishes the basic policies of the lottery and determines the types of games permitted. The executive director administers the day-to-day operations. In some states, this person is appointed by the governor; in others the director is appointed by the lottery commission. Commissioners are usually political appointees. Lottery staffs often include assistant directors who manage such activities as marketing, computer operations, and security (Commission on the Review of the National Policy toward Gambling, 1975).

Marketing ad sales are handled by private firms which bid competitively for a state contract. Different games may be under contract to different firms. Marketing the lottery is a unique operation for the state. Sophisticated techniques are required to maintain public interest and to compete with bordering states. Recognizing this fact, the Virginia lottery exempts future game information and some official records from the state's Freedom of Information Act. Virginia's lottery director cited competition with the District of Columbia and Maryland as the reason for the request (Anon., "VA Lottery Seeks . . .," 1988).

Marketing and sales staff are sometimes "donated" to state lottery agencies by private firms holding that state's lottery contract. Donated personnel reduce slightly the agency's direct costs, and thus the lottery appears to be a little cheaper to administer than it really is. Of course, the state pays anyway, in the form of higher prices for its contracted services.

State lottery commissions are the norm throughout the nation. Variations on some of these arrangements in Connecticut, Kentucky, and the Canadian provinces are worth noting. Connecticut combines administration of all forms of legal gambling—tele-track, jai alai, dogs, charity bingo games, and lotteries—into a single regulatory commission.

In Kentucky a public corporation runs lotteries. Kentucky legislation provides for a corporate-like structure designed to manage the lottery in an "entrepreneurial and businesslike manner." The lottery is headed not by a director, but by a president who has duties and powers similar to those of the chief executive officer in a corporation. As in Virginia, the "Kentucky Lottery Corporation" is permitted to hold closed meetings in order to protect trade secrets. The Kentucky statute also exempts all top management lottery employees from the state salary schedule and caps (Anon., "Kentucky Creates Unique . . .," 1989; Vance, 1986). Canadian provinces have a similar form of lottery organization, supposedly serving to keep lottery policy at arm's length from certain constraints imposed on other public agencies.

PRIVATIZATION

Some advocate the repeal of gambling prohibitions altogether. They recommend that the state relinquish its monopolistic control of this enterprise and permit private business firms to compete with each other in offering gambling services. It is said that in such an environment, states would not be forced to chose between citizens' welfare and revenue generation (Anon., "Economic Case Against . . .," 1975). Economist Milton Friedman is among the supporters of this change. Friedman explains that "when states operate numbers games they propagandize gambling and thus try to change people's values" (Anon., "Economic Case Against . . .," 1975).

Model proposals for privatization of lotteries take two forms. The "franchise" model would have each state draw elaborate specifications for conducting all phases of the games and award contracts to the highest bidder. The state payment would be in the form of a franchise tax— the difference between what the lottery raises and what the franchisee would be allowed to keep. The second, the NPO model, would turn over the games to non-profit organizations. They would receive lottery licenses on condition that the charities met state specifications. In fact, increasingly NPO raffles are now held in many states, as permitted under federal law.

Privatization removes a morally questionable enterprise from the direct sponsorship of the state. But the ever popular games would still be legal. This alternative, therefore, is viewed by some as a sort of permissible compromise between outright abolition and state promotion. Full privatization is the model advocated by Friedman. Full privatization still would require some considerable state regulation, but less than a franchise. Pressures from each private group to establish its own lottery would be immense. Arguably, the possibility for abuse would be greater if the lottery were in private hands. The need for state lottery agencies would continue, but their function would shift from primarily administrative to primarily regulatory. The lottery privatization idea has not proven to be a politically compelling one so far. A further analysis of the matter is reserved for the final chapter.

A comparison of these organizational structures appears in Table

Table 3.2. A Comparison of Types of State Lottery Organizational Structures and Characteristics.

State Agency	Public Corporation	Franchise Model	Full Privatization
Agency draws specifications for each game.	Major change from model one is in top control.	States' specifications for the games are drawn so that private firms keep profits from the games.	Multiple firms operate directly competing games.
Contracts with private firms for tickets, terminals, and marketing services.	Directors appointed for long terms (perhaps ten years or more).	Money left after prizes becomes the firm's profit (not a tax on winners).	Competition controls rates of profit and prizes.
After costs and prizes, remaining funds become profits (or "taxes") retained by state.	Policies are set and accountability mechanisms oriented to to the directors, not to the elected political leadership.	State payment is in the form of a "franchise fee" paid by the private firm for the right to operate a monopoly lottery.	State payment is in the form of a corporate profits tax.
	Profits flow to state as in model one.		

3.2. To the best of the writers' knowledge, models three and four are not implemented in the U.S. and Canada, and are therefore theoretical. They would have the political advantage of appearing to tax corporations that operate the games rather than to the players. Other than appearances, the differences are small. All structures envision a substantial profit for the state. This feature of contemporary state lotteries will be taken up again in Chapter 6.

LOTTERY FINANCES

In 1987 states returned between 41.8 percent (Missouri) and 57.5 percent (Massachusetts) of gross lottery sales as prizes to ticket holders (see Table 3.2). The proportion of total sales returned to players, referred to as the payoff or payout rate, is believed to be related to the success of the games (Hancock, 1987). Payout rates are sometimes limited by state statute. The average payoff rate for the twenty-three lotteries that operated in 1987 was 48.42 percent. However, the prize structure varies according to the particular lottery game, and usually averages a few percentage points below the advertised amount because of unclaimed prizes. In 1987 New York and New Jersey reported forfeited prizes of $19 million and $10 million respectively (various state Annual Reports for 1987). The 1987 payoff rate for each state is listed in Table 3.3.

Table 3.3. Finances of State Lotteries in Fiscal Year 1987.

State	Prizes as Percent of Sales (payoff rate)	Expenses as Percent of Total Revenue	Government Proceeds as Percent of Sales	Cents to Generate One Government Dollar
Arizona	44.70	19.09	35.62	53.59
California	48.79	15.01	36.20	41.46
Colorado	53.79	15.32	30.89	49.59
Connecticut	51.32	9.79	38.82	25.21
Delaware	51.94	10.82	37.24	29.07
District of Columbia	45.43	17.27	37.30	46.30
Illinois	49.46	8.90	41.64	21.38
Iowa	48.95	22.08	28.97	76.22
Maine	51.90	16.76	31.34	53.47
Maryland	48.23	8.07	43.70	18.47
Massachusetts	57.50	9.87	32.63	30.23
Michigan	45.60	13.95	40.45	34.49
Missouri	41.82	19.91	38.27	52.03
New Hampshire	49.44	16.24	34.32	47.32
New Jersey	48.78	8.92	42.32	21.08
New York	42.88	11.60	45.52	25.48
Ohio	50.72	14.14	35.14	40.24
Oregon	48.91	17.94	33.15	54.13
Pennsylvania	48.01	9.39	42.60	22.05
Rhode Island	46.49	16.24	37.27	43.56
Vermont	51.14	17.31	31.55	54.87
Washington	45.20	14.17	40.63	34.88
West Virginia	45.00	17.90	39.68	45.11
Average	48.42	14.38	37.18	40.01

Statistics computed from LaFleur (1988a).

The proportion of sales not returned to players is called the state's takeout rate. This figure includes net government revenues or state profit, and all administrative and operational expenses. Government proceeds, the most important statistic from the government's perspective, is the money remaining when all administrative and operational expenses have been deducted. On the average 37.18 percent of total lottery sales were retained by the states as profit in 1987. The net government revenue as a percent of total sales is shown by state in Table 3.3.

Lottery expenses are composed of agent commissions, consulting services from private industry firms, advertising, computer and instant vendor costs, salaries, and other expenses of the lottery staff. Like payout rates, maximum expense rates are sometimes specified by law. Table 3.3 indicates that expenses as a percent of total lottery revenues (ticket sales) ranged from a low of 8.1 percent in Maryland to a high of 22.1 percent in Iowa. Expenses in the twenty-three states which operated lotteries in 1987 averaged 14.38 percent of total lottery revenues.

When expenses are divided by government proceeds, the resultant figure is the ratio of expenses to net profits. This number also represents the number of cents spent to generate one government dollar, and it denotes the relative efficiency of a particular state lottery operation. The last column in Table 3.3 shows that in 1987 Maryland ran the most efficient lottery in that its expenses amounted to 18.5 percent of state lottery profits. In contrast, Iowa used 76.22 cents to raise one dollar in lottery profit.

Table 3.3 serves as a map for understanding the general financial structure of state lottery finances. The table shows that the portion of lottery sales returned to bettors, and the percentage of sales needed to maintain the lottery operation, vary considerably from state to state. More importantly, it illustrates that on the average, states must spend 40 cents to raise one dollar in lottery revenues. These figures are used by lottery administrators, industry analysts, and government officials in comparing states and guiding state lottery policy. We shall return to this table in the ensuing discussion of "lottery tax" efficiency.

REVENUE PERFORMANCE

The debate surrounding the lottery issue inevitably reaches the question of revenue potential. To aid in our discussion of lottery revenue

Table 3.4. Revenue Performance of State Lotteries, Fiscal Year 1987.

State	Total Lottery Revenues ($ millions)	Government Proceeds ($ millions)	Total Revenues as Percent of State Personal Income	Government Proceeds as Percent of State Own-Source Revenues
Arizona	$142.2	$50.7	.32%	1.2%
California	1,392.2	504.0	.31%	1.1%
Colorado	111.3	35.0	.23%	1.0%
Connecticut	489.3	189.9	.70%	3.3%
Delaware	45.8	17.1	.48%	1.2%
District of Columbia	121.7	45.4	1.02%	2.0%
Illinois	1,303.9	542.9	.72%	4.1%
Iowa	94.5	27.4	.25%	0.7%
Maine	58.1	18.2	.39%	1.1%
Maryland	760.5	332.4	1.01%	5.0%
Massachusetts	1,259.8	411.1	1.21%	3.9%
Michigan	1,006.3	407.1	.74%	3.1%
Missouri	174.4	66.7	.25%	1.3%
New Hampshire	60.2	20.7	.37%	2.0%
New Jersey	1,116.9	472.7	.79%	3.7%
New York	1,458.8	664.1	.48%	2.2%
Ohio	1,069.9	376.0	.71%	2.9%
Oregon	100.3	33.3	.28%	1.0%
Pennsylvania	1,338.5	570.2	.79%	4.0%
Rhode Island	57.9	21.6	.41%	1.3%
Vermont	25.3	8.0	.35%	1.0%
Washington	193.9	78.8	.29%	1.2%
West Virginia	70.6	28.0	.35%	1.2%
Total	12,454.3	4,931.1	.54%	2.2%

Lottery data from LaFleur (1988a). State revenue and income data from U.S. Bureau of the Census (1988a).

performance, 1987 state lottery figures are expressed in four different forms in Table 3.4.

In absolute terms, state lotteries collect large amounts of money. Total lottery revenues range from a low of $25.3 million in Vermont to a high of $1.4 billion in California. As Table 3.4 indicates, ticket sales in the nation's twenty-three lotteries totaled $12.4 billion; this represents a growth of 692 percent over the $1.7 billion sales figure of 1977.

Since state-operated lotteries are a thriving business, these total sales figures have enormous significance for the companies that produce scratch-off tickets and computer-run games. States generally pay these companies 2 to 5 percent of gross sales (Morain, 1987). When one considers that gross sales in many states exceed $1 billion, it is easy to understand the enthusiasm and fierce competition among the leading lottery corporations. Stock prices of these companies are sometimes affected when a new state approves a lottery.

In lottery campaigns, state proponents depend on these businesses for funding. Corporations that manufacture lottery equipment and operate lottery systems have a strong lobby, and have been a major impetus in the success of lottery legislation (Van de Kamp, 1984). For example, Scientific Games of Atlanta, Georgia, wrote California's 1984 lottery initiative, spent $2.1 million to persuade voters to pass it, and then signed a $20 million contract with the Golden State to produce instant game tickets (Morain, 1987). In the Florida lottery campaign, private industry spent approximately $600,000. GTECH of Providence, Rhode Island, spent approximately $125,000, while Scientific Games, a subsidiary of Bally Manufacturing, spent another $50,000. Neither company had been guaranteed a contract offer from the state (Morain, 1987). The lottery industry including tickets, advertising, and sophisticated computer equipment is, of course, worth billions of dollars.

Since game producers normally operate on commissions, total ticket sales is their prime concern. However, from a public finance perspective, total sales indicate little more than the amount of participation in the games. Government revenues, the money remaining after prize payouts, administrative costs, and commissions, is the more significant statistic. Of the $12.4 billion the lotteries collected in 1987, approximately $4.9 billion found its way into state coffers (see Table 3.4). While the revenue amounts are impressive in absolute terms, the cogent question remains. How important are lottery contributions to state government finance?

In discussing the relative performance of individual state lotteries, industry analysts (e.g., LaFleur, 1988a; Hancock, 1987) often compare lottery revenues to state personal income. According to LaFleur (1988a), "The percentage of a state's personal income spent on lottery games . . . more effectively addresses how efficient a lottery is with marketing to its player base [sales] and producing net income [government revenues]." Table 3.4 reveals that 1987 lottery revenues ranged in importance from a low of .23 percent of state personal income in Colorado to a high of 1.21 percent of state personal income in Massachusetts (LaFleur, 1988a; U.S. Bureau of the Census, 1988a). The Massachusetts figure suggests that, out of every thousand dollars in personal income, $12.10 was spent on the lottery. (The actual figure is somewhat lower, since the large Massachusetts jackpots attract many players from other New England states where lottery prizes are smaller.) Furthermore, the lottery industry is quick to point out that roughly half of the total wager is returned to bettors in the form of prizes.

Public sector analysts are more apt to consider lottery revenues in light of other state revenues. On average states with lotteries generate about 2.2 percent of their tax revenues from this source (see Table 3.4, last column). The larger percentages in Illinois, Maryland, and Pennsylvania are the exceptions. However, the statistics in the table exclude federal aid. When compared to total state revenue, with intergovernmental assistance included, the share is even less. In relative terms, some may consider lotteries to be a small portion of revenue generated by, or transferred to, state governments. However, since lotteries in ten states generated more revenue than alcohol or tobacco taxes, others would disagree.

Nevertheless, in comparison to sources that produce similar amounts, lotteries produce highly variable amounts of income from year to year (Mikesell and Zorn, 1987; Stewart, 1987). Weinstein and Deitch (1974) point out that states could generate the same amount of revenue by increasing sales tax rates by one-half of one percent. By virtue of their voluntary nature, narrow base, and high prize returns, lotteries are unable to match the revenue generated by direct taxes. Aronson et al. (1972) warn that lottery proceeds do not necessarily constitute new public funds. The purchase of lottery tickets precludes the expenditure of that money for taxable consumption of other goods and services.

WHO PAYS?

Opposition to lotteries is probably as old and enduring as the games themselves. The question of whether or not a state should institute a lottery usually stirs heated and emotional debate. The underlying conflict is waged on economic, political, and moral grounds. Adversaries and proponents invoke conflicting evidence. By and large, economists feel that state-run gambling is neither an efficient nor an equitable way to raise tax revenues. The popularity and ubiquity of lotteries suggest that voters and politicians disagree.

Economists generally evaluate taxes and revenue sources within the context of normative tax theory. Using normative criteria, some economists have determined that lotteries violate the conventional tax principles of vertical equity, efficiency, and neutrality (e.g., Borg and Mason, 1987; Brinner and Clotfelter, 1975; Clotfelter and Cook, 1987, 1989; Mikesell and Zorn, 1986; Rosen and Norton, 1966).

In tax theory, the principle of equity is one element of the incidence question which, when stated simply, asks, "Who pays the tax?" Vertical equity has to do with unequal tax treatment for unequals, or the ability to pay principle. The vertical equity or ability to pay principle states that "taxes should be distributed among taxpayers in relation to their financial capacities" (Aronson and Schwartz, 1981). In a regressive tax, the ratio of tax payments to income declines as income increases. In other words, individuals in lower income brackets spend a higher percentage of their income on taxes than do people in higher income ranges. Almost all economists who have studied the incidence of lotteries have concluded that the games are regressive. They warn that the poor and uneducated are the principal consumers, spending a greater proportion of their income on gambling than do better educated, wealthier people.

Lottery proponents argue that it is inappropriate to judge lotteries according to traditional tax criteria. They hold that lotteries are not really a tax but an entertainment commodity that consumers purchase voluntarily. Under this assumption, research pertaining to the regressivity, efficiency, or neutrality of lotteries is not germane (Sirkin, 1985). As Blakey (1979) states, "Taxpayers contribute to the government because they are forced to do so. . . . Bettors gamble, however, because they choose to do so." Furthermore, since they are voluntary, lotteries do not require the execution of tax forms, thereby reducing inconvenience to taxpayers.

Most impartial observers reject this argument. Using other excise taxes as examples, they argue that the taxes on liquor or tobacco products are no less a tax because citizens are not obligated to purchase these products. When the state establishes a legal monopoly, as is the case with lotteries and in some cases with liquor stores, the price burden on the buyer is the same as with other excise taxes. With lotteries the incidence of financing state services is distributed among consumers according to their participation in lotteries (Suits, 1979). Similarly, Brinner and Clotfelter (1975) state, "By allocating a portion of gross revenues for public use, state lotteries implicitly levy an excise tax on the purchase of lottery tickets." Clotfelter and Cook (1987) write, "While it is incorrect to conclude that 'lotteries are regressive,' the tax implicit in them certainly is." According to these authors, this implicit tax is levied at the average rate of 40 percent in the U.S.

In their economic analysis of state lotteries, Brinner and Clotfelter (1975) studied the incidence and regressivity questions with data based on a survey of 100 respondents in Massachusetts and 750 in Connecticut. They report that lottery expenditures rose to a peak in the middle income ranges and then declined. As a rule, families in the highest income groups spent slightly less than the lowest income cohort. In Connecticut, an income rise of 100 percent between the first and second income groups was accompanied by a 50 percent rise in lottery expenditures. In higher income groups, the absolute amounts of lottery expenditures fell. Brinner and Clotfelter (1975) concluded that "the excise tax inherent in the lottery is regressive throughout the income spectrum."

A study of the equity of state lotteries was conducted by the Sociology Department of the University of Connecticut. Professor Mark Abrahamson directed a study funded by the Connecticut State Commission on Special Revenues. The report concluded that the Connecticut lottery primarily attracts poor, unemployed, and less educated players. The study recommended the discontinuance of the lottery, claiming that it is a regressive means of raising state revenue (U.S. Senate, 1984).

In their 1987 study, Clotfelter and Cook attempted to determine the incidence of individual lottery games operated in California. They found that for weekly numbers games, expenditures as a percentage of income fall regularly with income, from 2.1 percent below $10,000 to 0.3 percent above $60,000. These researchers also found evidence of regressivity in the four-digit numbers and instant games. However, lotto games exhibited a pattern closer to proportionality. Only when jackpots rose beyond $5 million, did the incidence patterns become clearly progressive.

Considering states' tax structures as a whole, lotteries are more regressive than general sales, income, or property taxes. Thus the weight of Clotfelter and Cook's 1989 analysis is unmistakable. Overall the tax is regressive.

Previous studies that examined the equity of lotteries may be inconclusive because they failed to look at the state's uses of the funds or the demography of the beneficiaries. A telephone survey of 518 Illinois state lottery winners was designed to learn the characteristics of people who pay the games and to determine the extent to which these bettors received the educational benefits that are supposed to be enhanced by the earmarking of lottery revenues.

Total household lottery expenditures were regressed on selected demographic and socioeconomic variables. Lottery expenditures were higher in households where residents were older, non-white, had less formal education and lived in Chicago. Confirming other studies, this one found that lottery expenditures vary by income class. Lottery expenditures as a percentage of income fell throughout all the income categories (Borg and Mason, 1987). The lowest income groups spent the highest proportion of their income on tickets.

Other researchers (e.g., Heavey, 1978; Brinner and Clotfelter, 1975) also found that residents in the largest city in the state spent more for lottery tickets than other state residents. Since disproportionate numbers of poor people reside in the large cities, this high participation of city residents seems to confirm the notion that lottery taxes are regressive. Also, since non-whites are overrepresented among the poor, the finding that the non-white variable was a significant predictor of ticket purchase is also suggestive of tax regressivity.

Borg and Mason considered the "lottery tax" according to the "benefits received" principle. According to this principle, "Taxes are regarded as 'prices' and distributed in accordance with the estimated . . . benefits received by taxpayers from government goods and services." Borg and Mason constructed a model to determine the amount of direct benefit received by lottery players from education. They estimated the probability that the average household in the sample of lottery players would have a given number of children in public schools. Converting lottery revenue into amounts per student, they estimated the amount of direct benefit lottery-playing households received from public education. To determine the overall budgetary incidence, they subtracted this education benefit from the tax that the average lottery-playing household pays annually. Although consideration of the education benefits received tended to reduce the regressivity, Borg and Mason's (1987) research "reaffirms the conclusion that the excise tax inherent in a lottery is extremely regressive."

WHO PLAYS?

Analysis of tax incidence inevitably leads from a concentration on income to an examination of the social and demographic characteristics of citizens within income groups. For example, if lotteries prey upon the ignorance of players, it would be valuable to study the relationship between lottery participation and education. Concomitantly, race, age, gender, lifestyle, recent changes in one's circumstances, and psychological disposition have all been found to be determinants of lottery play. However, studies incorporating these variables often report conflicting findings.

Measurements based on raw expenditure data across income classes obscure an important element in lottery incidence: heavy participation is concentrated within a small subgroup of the population. A California survey asked residents about the number of tickets they had purchased over a two-month period. Only half the sample had purchased tickets. Responses revealed great variance in bets among players. The 8 percent of players who were the heaviest bettors were responsible for 60 percent of all purchases. The next 16 percent of the population bought another 20 percent of the tickets, leaving 80 percent of the population with little or no participation (Clotfelter and Cook, 1987, 1989).

This concentration of lottery play suggests that a small percentage of households in each income stratum contributes disproportionately to the lottery. In a comparison statement, Clotfelter and Cook (1987) conclude that "the dispersion in the tax burdens observed here is more pronounced at all income levels than for excise taxes in tobacco, gasoline, and telephones, and exceeds that for liquor."

Heavy lottery play is much more prevalent among blacks than whites. In the lowest income class, 41 percent of blacks reported betting more than $10 per week, compared to less than 8 percent for whites. Among whites, those with less than a high school education spend approximately $5 more per week than do college graduates (Clotfelter and Cook, 1987). Gambling is somewhat more prevalent among men (68 percent) than among women (55 percent) (Kantzer, 1983).

Gambling is learned early in life. Quebec, Canada was the site of a unique study. About 1,700 high school students were randomly surveyed from all social, academic, and ethnic strata. Seventy-six percent had gambled at least once in their lifetime; 24 percent gambled regularly; and 5.6 percent said they wanted to stop, but couldn't (Landocoeur and Mireault, 1988). Heavy play is also more prominent among the socially and economically distressed, whatever their social class. Those out of work, those who are stressed, those who have encountered a sudden reversal of fortune in money or in love are likely to gamble more than the rest of the population (Brenner and Brenner, 1990).

Devereux's (1980) classic study provides a broader explanation for much of the empirical evidence cited in this section. When conventional avenues of social mobility seem closed, people resort to more risky routes, such as lotteries. Odds are long, but they are the same odds for everyone. Knowledge, skill, personal contacts, prior history—distinctions that count in other parts of our lives—do not count insofar as lotteries are concerned. Every day is a fresh start. The poor, the elderly, those who feel discrimination, "count" just the same as anyone else. In this sense there is a certain transcendent equity in lotteries. Exclude the state's takeout and it's a very even playing field. Luck knows no social class. We elaborate these points in Chapter 6.

ILLEGAL ASPECTS

Illegal numbers games gross over $5.5 billion per year (Anon., "Leisure Time Industry," 1991). Legal lotteries have been advocated on the premise that they reduce participation in illegal games, diverting gambling to more honest state operations. The state maintains that it provides a gambling alternative outside the environment of illegal and often dishonest gambling operations. Officials reason that, since the amount of individual income that can be spent on gambling is fixed, the state games attract revenue from illegal operations.

Yet the data are ambiguous. The Commission on the Review of the National Policy toward Gambling (1975) reports that lotteries do, in fact, have an effect on illegal gambling activities. Hybels (1979) found that legalization increases utilization of illegal numbers games while possibly decreasing participation in entirely different forms of illegal gambling. Lottery officials in Rhode Island report that illegal numbers operations in that state were compelled to raise their payoff rates after lotteries were legalized. Similarly, vendors have received bribes to assist in the illegal numbers racket.

Blakey (1979) maintains that the games are not effective in diminishing the gambling operations of organized crime. Illegal numbers games are said to have the following advantages over the lotteries. "In illegal activities, players retain their anonymity; the Internal Revenue Service has no stake in the winnings; players and operators often share geographic, racial, and cultural commonalities" (Blakey, 1979). Others support this idea with claims that state games may have helped the illegal numbers business by reducing the stigma of playing.

Suits (1979) maintains that in order for the state to raise revenues with lotteries, it must maintain a condition in which illegal gambling is also profitable. This means that the state must be in competition with illegal games; it must offer competitive odds and payoffs. Legal lotteries may pull players from illegal sports books or dice games, but they may also prompt an increase in numbers (Hybels, 1979).

STUDIES ARGUING FOR LEGALIZATION

Government and industry proponents cite evidence which suggests that lotteries do not prey upon society's unfortunates. In his testimony before the U.S. Senate Subcommittee on Intergovernmental Relations, Martin Puncke (1984) invoked the following statistics. More whites than non-whites (62 percent versus 52 percent) bet on the state lottery. Low income groups show lower participation rates than higher income groups (24 percent for those with household income of less than $5,000, compared to 74 percent for those over $15,000). Participation rises uniformly with education, from 41 percent for those with less than a high school education to 79 percent for those who have completed college.

Hancock (1987) also refutes the notion that the poor purchase a disproportionate amount of lottery tickets. According to him, studies in several states show that the highest level of participation comes from lower-middle and middle income persons. He also cites a California study that incidates that the most active players earn good wages. In a final argument Hancock points out a third study conducted in Michigan, indicating that most active players are likely to be fully employed in a skilled, semiskilled, or trade occupation.

Dr. John Koza (1987), co-founder of the lottery company Scientific Games, examined the household income and lottery expenditure profiles of 140 winners. Games were run by the states of New York, Pennsylvania, Illinois, Michigan, and New Jersey. Participation in individual games was highest among middle income households. He concluded, "The 'poor' participate in the state lottery games at levels disproportionately less than their percentage of the population." He failed to find a single case where lower income groups participated at a rate even equal to their percentage in the population.

Shippee et al. (1983) found no evidence of regressivity. These researchers found a close correspondence between the median income of lottery players and the median household income of Arizona residents.

State lottery commissions sometimes include the results of lottery player research in their annual reports or other promotional materials. A recent demographic study in Colorado indicates that the average player is "between the ages of twenty-five and forty-four years old (48 percent), has a high school education and some college (68 percent)" (Colorado State Lottery, 1988). Typical players earned between $15,000 and $35,000 annually in the mid-1980s. Seventeen percent earned between $35,000 and $49,999.

The more recent findings of McConkey and Warren (1987) tend to reinforce proponents' assertions that lotteries do not prey on the poor. McConkey and Warren employed multiple discriminant function analysis to profile lottery players along psychographic and demographic dimensions. Their subjects were purchasers of lottery tickets in all lottery states: 1,651 respondents completed a mail questionnaire. Information requested pertained to lifestyle, shopping and purchasing patterns, and demographic and socioeconomic characteristics.

Respondents were segmented into three groups: heavy purchasers, light purchasers, and non-purchasers. The findings tend to contradict some of widely held assumptions among scholars (e.g., Brinner and Clotfelter, 1975; Clotfelter, 1979; Kaplan, 1984; Suits, 1977) that players are poor, uneducated, and unemployed. Their discriminant function analysis led McConkey and Warren to the conclusion that,

> Purchasers tend to be more active, optimistic individuals with modern or more liberal attitudes. They tend to be in the younger middle ages, at least moderately well educated, have employed spouses, and reside in

urban areas. They are not poor, and in fact, they tend to have above average incomes.

In connection with the finding that some purchasers are optimistic individuals by nature, it is interesting to note the remergence of published pamphlets and lists of lucky numbers. A new form of the old "Dream Books," the pamphlets rely on highly modern statistical computing techniques. Essentially the computational task is to distinguish between popular and unpopular combinations of numbers. Unpopular number combinations are considered good bets: winners are statistically less likely to have to share winnings with other ticket holders.

Relying on such approaches does indeed represent an optimistic attitude—unbounded optimism. The chances of winning substantial amounts of money at lottery play is so small that no consistent lottery player can hope to break even. (It has been calculated that the chances of being struck by lightning are greater.) Besides, if unpopular number combinations become widely known, they will receive more play.

These empirical investigations of the lottery illustrate a dilemma increasingly recognized by social scientists. The data are often conflicting, and may in fact be produced by interested parties. Numbers become a mode of argumentation rather than a clear indicator of truth.

For many, the regressivity of the lottery remains the most important question. Academic studies are nearly unanimous in condemning the games as regressive. Research conducted by private industry advocates, reported by state lottery commissions or in trade magazines indicate otherwise.

ADMINISTRATIVE EFFICIENCY

As a fund-raising device, the state lottery is also criticized as being deplorably inefficient (e.g., Blakey, 1979; Borg and Mason, 1987; Mikesell and Zorn, 1986; Rosen and Norton, 1966; Anon., "Economic Case Against . . .," 1975; Thomas and Webb, 1984). According to Aronson and Schwartz (1981), tax efficiency "concerns the 'convenience and compliance costs' to the taxpayers to determine and pay their tax liability, in addition to the costs to the taxing unit to collect taxes." Inefficiency in taxation suggests excess costs to the taxpayer and taxing jurisdiction.

In the section on lottery finances, it was explained that 42 to 57 percent of gross lottery revenues are paid out in prizes. When expenses of 8 to 22 percent are added, states are left with a profit of between 29 and 45 percent. Table 3.3 indicated that if lotteries are considered a tax, they are an inefficient one indeed. Maryland, which operates the most efficient lottery, spends 18 cents to produce one dollar of net revenue. Iowa invests 76 cents to generate one dollar of government revenue. On the average, the twenty-two lottery states and the District of Columbia spent 40 cents to raise one dollar in 1987.

Viewed as a tax, lotteries are incredibly costly to administer. Yet there are no taxes quite similar to lotteries, which market a "product" with very minimal costs of production. If casino gambling, for example, were run by state governments instead of private industry, the number of cents expended to raise one tax dollar would be even higher than for lotteries. Most of a casino's gross handle is paid back to winners, show girls, and entertainers, etc. If state liquor stores were to include wholesale cost of liquor and advertising as part of the "cost to raise one dollar," excise taxes on alcohol would be dubbed woefully inefficient. In part, then, the tax inefficiency of lotteries is due to unique accounting and marketing arrangements and the fact that all aspects of the product are state owned.

A more compelling indictment of lotteries on efficiency grounds is the one against government's high takeout rate. Playing poker or roulette offers a much greater chance of winning than playing the lottery. Does this high "tax" on lotteries, in comparison to other forms of gambling, reduce propensity to play? Obviously, if the state kept every dollar spent on lottery tickets no one would play the lottery. If it returned every dollar to players, the state would have no reason to conduct one. If the object is to raise maximum revenues by encouraging play, what payout rate would do it?

The authors are not suggesting this should be the states' aim. We are simply pointing out that little experimentation on this matter has been conducted by state lottery agencies. In fact states are far from anxious to discuss the financial returns to players.

A second efficiency question has to do with the effects of gambling on the productivity of society. Does gambling discourage work as its detractors assert, merely redistributing the wealth we already have? Or does gambling produce new wealth by giving people one more pleasurable, leisure time activity?

To the writers' knowledge, the broad question has not been investigated empirically. However, a much more limited question has been investigated. Do lotteries affect spending on other forms of gambling? And does establishment of other forms of gambling affect expenditures on lotteries? These questions become significant as more and more jurisdictions consider additional legalizations. Summarizing the research briefly, new forms of gambling within a particular locale reduce expenditures on the old forms, but by much less than 100 percent. The old forms remain profitable and the society simply devotes more resources to gambling, in the aggregate.

Addition of new gambling forms has been estimated to impact government revenues in heretofore unforseen ways. If, say, casino gambling with a low takeout rate is legalized along with lotteries where the government's take is especially high, there could be what economists call a "negative net revenue effect." Government may end up with less money after additional games are legalized than it had before (Gulley and Scott, 1989; Vache, 1990).

LOTTERIES AND CONSUMER SPENDING BEHAVIOR

Some critics hold that lotteries also fall short on a third criterion for tax evaluation—neutrality. According to Jones (1985), a neutral tax "should not interfere with individual saving and consumption preferences." With a neutral tax, "consumers spend their income remaining after taxes in the same way they would have if they had had the same amount of money before the tax was imposed." Economists wonder about the questionable role of government lotteries in regard to individual consumption decisions. With lottery advertising and public relations currently running over $635 million, it appears that lotteries clearly do affect consumer spending patterns.

The advertisement of lottery products could have important effects on the behavior and attitudes of citizens. Stocker (1972) further develops this idea when he writes,

> Let us assume that there is nothing morally reprehensible about gambling. . . . There is a world of difference between a government stance of neutrality regarding gambling and one of active promotion. There is no other form of consumption that receives such an official encouragement. The nearest examples . . . are library services and adult education both of which are examples of merit wants, which gambling is not.

> In the closest other examples of state operated commercial activity, the liquor monopolies, states have usually been reticent about promoting their wares. In the lottery . . . we are seeing for the first time government sanctioning one form of private personal consumption over others . . . this raises serious questions as to the proper role of government in regard to individual consumption decisions.

The question of tax neutrality may be more significant than the regressivity issue. With reference to the neutrality criterion, Weinstein and Deitch (1974) ask the following salient questions. Should the state encourage its citizens to buy a particular good in preference to others? Should consumption choices be influenced only by the private marketplace? Does not the prohibition of lotteries interfere with freedom of consumers to spend money on what they want?

This section discussed state lotteries with respect to their purported violations of normative tax theory. If one makes the assumption that the lottery constitutes or contains an implicit tax, it seems reasonable to believe that it is an inefficient one. The literature also indicates that lottery games are very regressive. Given the extent of lottery advertising and promotion, in relation to other state commodities, many will agree that this "voluntary tax" influences consumer spending. Given the state's monopolistic control over lotteries, its influence on consumers violates the principle of tax neutrality.

A POTPOURRI OF ETHICAL CONSIDERATIONS

Statistics are used to demonstrate and answer both sides of what is to many essentially a moral question. Objections to state lotteries extend beyond the context of tax theory and into the realm of ethics and political policy. Here, advocates and adversaries invoke more practical arguments in supporting their positions.

According to Brinner and Clotfelter (1975), "The most realistic model of the state lottery is that of a monopoly, except that monopoly profits are now called tax revenues." State officials view lotteries as an entertainment product. In order for this monopolistic "entertainment business" to achieve continued success, the products must be marketed aggressively. It has been well established that promotion and product change is vital to the success of lotteries (Hancock, 1987). *Gaming and Wagering Business* reports that in 1988, states spent approximately $188 million on advertising (Anon., "U.S. Lottery . . .", 1988).

Lottery critics are generally opposed to the idea of government-sponsored gambling. What is more, they are vehemently opposed to the aggressive marketing by the state. They contend that publicly financed state lottery advertising is inconsistent and contrary to the goals of state government. For example, Sarasohn (1983) writes,

> Implicit in any government's explanation of why it takes money from its citizens, is the idea that taxes are the price paid for civilization. The force of that argument and the public atmosphere are somehow eroded by the addendum, "You could win big."

In *The New Republic,* Marshall (1978) comments, "States set out to control gambling by monopolizing it, but in the process they have become hooked on the vice themselves."

Objections are made to the variety of gimmicks states use to create excitement. The general feeling among lottery opponents is that states hold out false hope to people by promoting games with astronomical odds. Odds of winning are underadvertised, while prizes are not quoted in present values but as prizes distributed over the period of years. Critics claim that these practices, which would be unlawful in the private sector, constitute dubious state policy. In *The New Republic,* Elliott Marshall maintains, "If citizens peddled false hopes as state governments do, they'd be in jail."

People recognize that lotteries have become the most popular form of legalized gambling. The proximity of lottery tickets, they say, makes gamblers out of former non-gamblers. Low ticket prices and heavy advertising entice people to purchase lottery tickets with their newspapers and groceries (Anon., "Many States Find . . ., 1988).

Lotteries create a moral dilemma for states. With the games, states allow and entice people to engage in previously forbidden activities. This decriminalization of gambling behavior generates revenue, without raising conspicious taxes. This use of lotteries has been called a kind of "fiscal avoidance behavior" (Sarasohn, 1983). Brinner and Clotfelter (1975) observe, "We have a paradox of a regressive tax with social gain. . . . In economic terms, an efficiency gain is realized through the joint creation and taxation of a new consumer good."

Acknowledging the relative insignificance of lottery revenues and the possible social costs of gambling, Frey (1984) offers this view.

> It is the job of our legislators to address forthrightly the critical issues confronting our society today. Lotteries and other forms of legalized gambling obfuscate these issues by impeding progress toward their

amelioration. If they are used as escape mechanisms and painless methods of revenue generation, they will have a negative influence on society. They appear as red herrings in a sea populated by a plethora of political jellyfish without the backbone to confront the unpopular but necessary issues of tax reform, fiscal responsibility, and long-range planning—the only ways sufficient funds can be generated to cope with the monumental problems of crime, energy, poverty, health, education. . . .

Supporters maintain that government policy must reflect social realities. Pragmatists argue that gambling is a deep-seated human want which people will satisfy regardless of the government's stance. The parallel between alcohol prohibition and lotteries is often cited. Many considered prohibition to be a great moral cause, but lack of public support made the law virtually unenforceable. Industry and state leaders argue that gambling is a natural desire which, like alcohol consumption, cannot be stopped by legislation.

Smith and Abt (1984) offer credibility to this opinion. They state that games are among the rituals by which individuals are socialized into a culture. In America, materialism and competition are two distinguishing traits which are reflected in our games. Smith and Abt speculate that "such games may actually predispose Americans to gambling behavior." They add that "it is not surprising that commercial gambling among adults has become . . . a significant social, economic, and cultural issue in contemporary American civilization."

Are lotteries and other forms of gambling to be discouraged simply because they appeal to the poor, the destitute, those down on their luck? The Brenners (Brenner and Brenner, 1990) offer their view that "it is not true that gamblers are either mentally ill or criminals and this is why they become poor. Rather it is the other way around: the poor and the frustrated gamble." The games provide hope, relief from grief and anxiety to the desperate, and harmless recreation to the vast majority. The solution is not prohibition of gambling but greater social justice.

Others agree. For example, Stocker (1972) expresses a similarly libertarian attitude.

> The moralists indulge in the time-honored American custom of passing judgement on the actions of others and if possible enacting their own moral code into law. Such a position not only offends against personal liberty, but also runs counter to the general economic rule that the individual consumer is the best judge of his own welfare and that he

should be allowed the widest possible lattitude in his consumption decisions, as long as they do not harm someone else (i.e., create negative ex-
ternalities). By this reasoning the moralistic argument must be rejected.

On the other side are those who argue that lotteries increase gambling behavior. They are bothered by the endurance of gambling behavior in hard economic times. Research for the Commission on the
Review of the National Policy toward Gambling indicates that the increased availability of gambling opportunities leads to greater participation. Phalon (1984) comments, "Recession in the form of steel and
auto cutbacks hit hard in such states as Ohio and Michigan without putting a dent in the lottery fender." According to Richard Richardson of
the Maryland Council on Compulsive Gambling, lotteries have created
"new classes of compulsive gamblers—women and teens" (Shapiro,
1988).

To date there has been no link between legal lotteries and widespread
criminal behavior on the part of state officials, major vendors, or the
corporations that are involved in the business of providing tickets and
computer hardware. A rise in crime against property—especially
embezzlement and robbery—has been associated with the presence of
a lottery in a state (Colson, 1987; Mikesell and Pirog-Good, 1990).

Frey (1984) reports that in New Jersey, the number of people seeking
help for compulsive gambling has increased dramatically since the
legalization of casinos in Atlantic City. Events such as this prompt a
minimal level of state action. In Iowa, one-half of one percent of lottery
revenues is dedicated to the "Gambler's Assistance Fund" which provides programs that deal with the problem of compulsive gambling
(Iowa Lottery, 1988). A New Jersey statute requires that $75,000 per
year be allocated for compulsive gambling studies. That state's lottery
officials have begun placing labels on the 4,500 lottery machines in the
state. The labels advise players to call 1-800-GAMBLER for help if
they or someone they know has a gambling problem.

These activities, however, are always a compromise worked out to
forestall more substantial legislation or systematic study. The dimensions of the serious gambling problem are unknown, even in Nevada
where casinos have operated since the Great Depression. William
Eadington (1984), one of the nation's leading authorities on gambling,
writes,

At present the understanding of the incidence of compulsive gambling and the degree of severity it manifests in those afflicted is insufficient for the creation of reasonable public policies to deal with the problem. The second issue deals with the potential for curing the pathological gambler. Here again the evidence is quite sketchy.

We have seen that in past centuries lotteries were denounced on both religious and secular moral grounds. Today's debate lends slightly new perspectives to the age old issues. Some speculate that since significant numbers of people believe that gambling is categorically wrong, decriminalization or legalization "makes allegiance to government extremely difficult for people with deep moral convictions" (Commission on the Review of the National Policy toward Gambling, 1976). Government must weigh the cost to the majority against the benefits to the majority. The commission also held that the effect of legalizing or decriminalizing gambling on the work ethic is impossible to determine. They acknowledged, however, that government may be undermining the work ethic by allowing or encouraging citizens to make a profit through chance rather than through work.

According to Richard Phalon (1984), "The lottery in all its forms is a sucker's game with a risk-reward ratio far worse than horse racing and casino gambling." In an attempt to summarize moralists' opposition to lotteries, John Ezell (1960) invokes the words of Sir William Petty that,

> It is not fit that every man that will, may cheat every man that would be cheated. Rather it is ordained that the sovereign should have guard of these fools, even as in the case of lunatics and idiots.

Petty was speaking about lotteries. His admonitions seem to apply equally well today.

CONCLUSION

A century ago lottery criticism was focused on fraud, default, and bribery. Spectacular examples of abuse were widespread. People, especially the poor, developed unreal expectations, a tendency toward crime, and, allegedly, an irreverent attitude toward honest labor. The poor overindulged in the games. In 1960, Ezell wrote, "The most careful supervision cannot eradicate the inevitable abuses in a system particularly susceptible to fraud."

No one could have foreseen how computer technology would eliminate a major, if not the most important, source of lottery criticism. Computer applications together with government sponsorship have improved public trust to the degree that the possibility of fraud is no longer a real concern. It seems reasonable to assume that, had nineteenth century lotteries been as impervious to fraud and abuse as today's games, federal and state government would not have imposed the sixty-nine-year period of lottery abolition.

While lottery integrity is not currently an issue, objections on moral, economic, social, and political grounds persist. The games prey upon the poor and the weak. Allegedly they may lead to an increase in other forms of gambling, or in compulsive gambling. However, most of the current criticism seems to focus on economic and political considerations rather than moral ones. Social scientists argue that the lottery is a tax, and a very regressive one. They argue that the large takeout rate cannot be justified on sumptuary grounds, given the extensive marketing practices of state lottery agencies. They question the propriety of this state-sponsored gambling for economic and political reasons.

Important for the purposes of this study is the claim that specific programs that are targeted in lottery campaigns do not receive enhanced or more stable funding. Blakey (1979) notes that the value of the lottery can only be determined by a "thoughtful balancing of all its economic, political, social, and moral implications." The preceding discussion of lottery operations and issues facilitates an understanding of the broad implications involved in using lotteries to raise government revenues for education or other public functions. Policy makers and educators can use this understanding, in conjunction with the ensuing statistical analyses, to develop their stance on lottery, and "lottery-for-education" initiatives.

CHAPTER 4

A Framework for Analyzing Lottery Revenues

THE previous chapters established the lottery as an historic, controversial, popular, and increasingly important source of public finance. Social scientists and policy analysts warn, however, that lotteries are dubious social policy (e.g., Blakey, 1979; Brinner and Clotfelter, 1975; Mikesell and Zorn, 1986; Suits, 1977). Moreover, educators fear that the political link between school funding and lotteries has an overall pernicious effect on public school finance. They warn that the political-fiscal connection between lotteries and education desensitizes the citizenry to school finance crises and makes the education of American youth partially dependent on an unreliable revenue source (e.g., Hartwig, 1987; Shapiro, 1988; Sirkin, 1985; Stewart, 1987; Thomas and Webb, 1984).

This chapter presents a research method for viewing lotteries in light of public expenditure theory. A framework is offered for analyzing the impact of lotteries on the fiscal provisions for public schools in the American states.

The initiation of the study was based on three concerns. First is the fact that lotteries are themselves as contentious as the taxes they try to avoid. Many warn that lotteries are unhealthy public policy. Second, lottery advocates purport that lotteries enhance support for education, while some educators take a diametrically opposite position. Third, there is a need for additional data which educators and officials can use to support or rebuff proposals linking school finance with state lotteries. A review of additional research supporting our model appears in Appendix A.

LOTTERIES AND SCHOOL FINANCE:
STATE CASE STUDIES

In this section we focus directly on the relationship between lotteries and school finance. We review case studies which examine the "lottery-education connection" in individual states. These few studies deal with the major question of this book, do lotteries enhance education revenues? However, these works neither addressed the overall impact of lotteries on a national or aggregate level, nor did they attempt to determine whether the characteristics of specific lotteries, which vary from state to state, determine public school funding.

In a paper sponsored by Policy Analysis for California Education, Eric Hartwig (1987) discussed the problems of the lottery-education program in California. After presenting in-depth information on the development and other aspects of the state lottery's education provisions, Hartwig reported the results of a survey that was distributed to eighty-eight superintendents throughout California. The superintendents were asked to provide three types of data.

> quantitative data regarding the uses of lottery revenue, additudinal information that could be measured quantitatively, and qualitative data concerning the respondents' experiences with and attitudes towards the lottery program.

The salient results of the survey are presented below.

(1) Superintendents indicated that they were "prudent" in spending the lottery revenue; only 24 percent of the money had been spent. Hartwig (1987) concluded that, since the lottery was in its first year, most districts were assuming a wait-and-see approach, "so that they would not be hostage to unknown or fluctuating lottery revenues."

(2) The attitudinal data were similar in substance and tone to repeated admonitions of some educators and state officials around the nation. One of the survey questions had to do with the perceived stability of lottery funds. The majority (61.3 percent) felt that the lottery income would decline. Approximately 28 percent thought that lottery revenues to their districts would fluctuate.

(3) More importantly for this study, approximately 90 percent of those who responded agreed that the lottery would have an adverse impact on the legislature's willingness to fund educational programs.

However, it is interesting to note that the responses of superintendents in districts with per pupil expenditures less than the state average, were significantly different from those of chief officials in districts spending above the state mean. Hartwig added that not only were poorer districts spending more of their lottery money on basic supplies, they were "more pessimistic about the long-term outlook for sustained state support for education programs."

The vast majority of respondents said they supported legislation stipulating that lottery revenues be considered a supplement to rather than a substitution for established sources of education finance. Although such language was enacted in October of 1985, superintendents' apprehension about the effectiveness of such language was reflected in the survey.

Hartwig surmised that despite specific statutory language labeling lottery funds as supplementary, not all administrators saw it that way. Administrators were torn between pressures to restore badly eroded basic programs and pressures to provide truly new services enhancing public education (Hartwig, 1987).

Many of the superintendents described how the lottery money had provided additional enhancements and embellishments to their districts. They cited extras such as increased library book purchases, fine arts supplies, extra personnel for special needs, and augmented summer school programs. But after listing the "enhancements," many respondents added that the lottery was helping to compensate for years of underfunding. Hartwig concluded that this "enhancement" issue was largely a question of semantics. In his words,

> This is not to say that some uses, such as establishment of scholarship funds, sending sixth graders to science camp, financing field trips, and outfitting bands and athletic teams, aren't true "enhancements" to a district's educational program. Rather, whether a particular use of lottery revenue augments the normal educational program depends on the point of view of the superintendent and on the history of the district. To one superintendent, providing a microscope for every two students in a science class where before the school had one for every four students is an enhancement; to another it would be "catching up."

Many superintendents expressed concern about whether or not all the publicity surrounding the lottery's benefit to schools would create the mistaken idea that education funding left little to be desired. By stressing the Lottery Act's emphasis on the enhancing nature of the revenues, districts' uses of lottery funds for visible, high-impact, supplemental programs could give taxpayers the impression that the basics are under control. Superintendents worried about the long-term implications that could result if this misconception were to become widespread.

Thus, this report entitled, "Do Our Schools Win, Too?" elucidates some important issues which arise under a state policy to fund public education with gambling money. The "supplement or substitution" question is avoided because of the difficulties involved in measuring the precise impact of lottery funds, or for that matter, any specifically earmarked revenues to public education. Even with legislation designed to insure "additive effects" of lottery profits, the interaction of limited resources, financial history, and changing needs of school districts, results in largely unforeseen and immeasurable, fungible effects of this "additional money." Although Hartwig's research concerned California, it seems reasonable that attempts to determine the specific impact of lottery-education programs in other states where lottery revenues are earmarked, would be plagued by similar, confounding factors.

California had enacted its lottery only one year prior to Hartwig's data collection. Respondents expressed concern that the highly visible lottery money would become an important factor in employee salary negotiations. Superintendents were also apprehensive about using lottery revenues for other recurring costs such as insurance, and maintenance contracts. One implication is that to the extent lotteries are truly supplemental, those supplements are likely to occur in the first years of the lottery's operation, before the state-local revenue structure has had time to adjust to the influx of lottery dollars.

It is important to note that school district leaders in California were very apprehensive about funding their schools with lottery profits. This finding reinforces the opinions of others who flay education-lottery programs. It highlights the paradoxical situation that confronts educators in California and in other states where citizens are told that the lottery helps schools. On the one hand, educators praise the programs and purchases made possible through the lottery. Yet, on the other hand, they know that they may be reinforcing the perception among taxpayers and legislators that lottery monies are not commingling with regular funding.

Stewart (1987) analyzed the effects of earmarked lottery revenue for public elementary and secondary education in New York and Michigan. Her study was structured around the following two questions.

(1) Did lottery revenue generated in these two states prove to be a stable, reliable, high-yield source of revenue?
(2) Did available data support the claim that net lottery revenues contribute to the expansion of the functional area of public elementary and secondary education?

Employing an interrupted time-series design, Stewart collected data (for a period five years before the intervention of the lottery through 1985) at the end of each fiscal year. To adjust for inflation, actual dollars were converted to constant dollars using the Consumer Price Index (CPI) base 1986. Visual images of trends in revenue and expenditure patterns were presented with graphs prepared using the Lotus 1-2-3 spread sheet.

To determine the stability, reliability, and significance of lottery revenue, Stewart examined and compared total and per capita revenue from state lotteries, state income tax, state sales tax, and property tax by state. In absolute terms, net state revenues derived from lotteries were significant in both states. However, when expressed as a percent of total own source revenue, the lottery amounted to 3.23 percent in Michigan and 2.37 percent in New York.

Per capita lottery income in New York rose from $1 in 1976 to $34 in 1985; in Michigan it increased from $12 to $45 in the same period. When actual dollar amounts were transformed into constant dollars, significant fluctuations were noted. For example, in 1976, the Michigan lottery generated $23 per capita. In 1980, the figure rose to $31 per capita, but declined to $27 in 1983. A similar pattern is seen in New York, where adjusted revenues of $7 per capita in 1973, and $8 in 1979, fell to $6 in 1980.

Stewart found lotteries to be an unstable source of revenue. Between 1980 and 1981, for example, Michigan's lottery suffered a nearly 10 percent decline. From 1984 to 1985 lottery revenues increased by 46.79 percent. An unpredictable pattern is also evident in New York. Occasional yearly decreases in net lottery revenue should not obscure their sizable growth long term. For example, in 1969 and 1977, the New York lottery saw real net growth of 193.9 percent and 280.3 percent, respectively.

Unstable source of revenue

In contrast to lotteries, more conventional forms of tax revenue were much more significant and stable. During the period studied, Michigan saw only one decrease in growth of total state tax revenue, which amounted to − 1.16 percent in 1980. State sales tax receipts declined by .83 percent in 1975 and by 9.12 percent in 1976. Unadjusted state income tax revenue experienced declines of 12.35 percent and 9.91 percent in 1975 and 1985, respectively. Similar to Michigan, New York experienced a much more constant yield of revenues from conventional taxes than it did from the lottery. New York experienced no negative changes in the percent of growth of its total state tax or state sales tax revenue. Unadjusted income tax figures show slight declines of .40 percent in 1965, .62 percent in 1973, and a drop of .46 percent in 1978.

Lotteries, then, are subject to fluctuations in the business cycle, changing consumer preferences, and competition from neighboring state lotteries. Furthermore, as pointed out in Chapter 3, lotteries provide a very limited tax base. At best they can make up a small portion of total own source state revenue.

To answer her second question, Stewart examined the fiscal condition of the state system of public elementary and secondary education in Michigan and New York, through the following indices.

(1) State direct education expenditures as a percent of state direct general expenditures: Michigan, fiscal years 1967–1985, and New York, fiscal years 1963–1985

(2) Per pupil public school expenditures: Michigan, 1967–1986, and New York, 1962–1986

(3) Average teacher salaries: Michigan, 1967–1986, and New York, 1962–1986

Stewart hypothesized that if lottery revenues were not fungible, the percent of total direct general expenditures accounted for by education would increase. She found that, after earmarking, direct education expenditures as a percent of total state direct expenditures declined in New York, and only increased .06 percent in Michigan.

Average teacher salaries and per pupil expenditures were employed by Stewart as additional measures of the fiscal growth of the public education systems in New York and Michigan. As expressed in CPI base 1986 dollars, the average annual growth in per pupil expenditures in Michigan before the intervention of the lottery was 5.58 percent; average annual growth during the earmark period was 2.22 percent. The average annual growth in per pupil expenditures in New York before earmarking was 4.97 percent; during the earmarking period it declined to 3.24 percent.

When adjusted to CPI base 1986 dollars, average teacher salaries exhibited a similar trend. Before the dedication of lottery revenue to public education, the average annual percent change in teacher salaries was 4.28 in Michigan (1968–1981) and 1.86 in New York (1963–1976). Since schools had become the designated recipients of lottery profits, this percent change decreased to 1.60 in Michigan (1982–1986) and fell to − .13 percent in New York (1977–1986).

Since both are used to fund public schools, Stewart also compared the growth of lottery revenue and property taxes in the two states. Before lottery revenue was earmarked for education, property tax in Michigan grew at the average annual rate of 4.13 percent. In the years following the dedication of lottery revenue (1982–1985), property taxes had increased at the average annual rate of 3.50 percent. Before lottery dedication (1962–1976), property taxes in New York experienced an average growth of 13.57 percent annually. These revenues declined at an average annual rate of 26.3 percent during the years when lottery profits were earmarked for public education (1977–1985).

Stewart concluded that,

> If lottery funds are not fungible, expenditures in earmarked functional categories would be expected to increase due to the additional revenues being generated by a lottery. . . . Claims made by lottery proponents that net lottery revenues contribute to the expansion of the functional area of public elementary and secondary education are not supported by data analyzed for Michigan and New York.

Unlike Borg and Mason (1987, 1990), whose research is reviewed below, Stewart did not apply statistical tests per se to determine the significance of trends and relationships; her conclusions were reached based on the visual examination of graphic and tabular data. This simplicity in technique notwithstanding, Stewart's hypotheses and conclusions seem plausible.

However, factors that threaten internal validity in most time-series designs (Campbell and Stanley, 1963) may have also been operating in Stewart's research. These are discussed toward the end of this section.

Stewart's examination is not the only one dealing with the question of fungibility of school lottery revenues. Borg and Mason (1987, 1990) employed trend analysis in an attempt to detect significant differences in support for education in Illinois, before and after the dedication of lottery funds for schools.

These economists observed that states do not have policies "to preclude the diversion of funds which would have gone to education from being diverted to other programs" (Borg and Mason, 1987). Obviously, this fact has enormous significance for educators and policymakers. Borg and Mason reported that while lottery revenues to education had skyrocketed, state funding was increasing at a much lower rate than it had in the pre-lottery years. Statistical tests revealed significant differences in the trend of state support to education after the implementation of the Illinois lottery. The authors conclude,

> The lottery has led to a decline in allocations to education without the benefits of tax relief. These results . . . certainly represent a funding scheme that the voters of Illinois did not approve and one that they may not be aware is occurring. As a result of these findings, the only conclusion that can be drawn is that lotteries which are designated to support education, in all likelihood, do not . . . there is no reason to believe that other specific programs designated as lottery fund recipients are any more likely to be truly supported by the lottery funds.

Employing more sophistication in statistical technique, Borg and Mason confirm the findings of Stewart, that lottery funds are very fungible. These results adduce the fears in the education community, that the lottery has long-range deleterious effects on public school finance.

A 1991 study by Stark, Honeyman, and Wood examined two issues in connection with the Florida lottery, first implemented in 1987. The first question was: "Are lottery revenues supplemental or substitutive?" This had been the subject of the two prior studies. Using linear regression Stark et al. found that the lottery did not lead to overall funding enhancement. Some of Stark's analyses confirmed the findings of Stewart (1987) and Borg and Mason (1987). School revenues had not grown at the normal incremental rate in Florida in the year after the lottery was enacted. Data can be interpreted to show that lotteries are a drag on education funding rather than a stimulus.

It is well settled that the state's share of total school revenues affects the equity of spending. That is, the greater the portion of spending provided through state funds, the more equal the spending across local districts tends to be. Making the same point differently, states with low percentages of local funding per pupil tend to be more equitable. Conceptually, lotteries which impact the over-all levels of state school aid, up or down, would also effect the distribution of those revenues.

Stark, Honeyman, and Wood's second research question is unique in that no other researchers had posited it previously: "Does the lottery affect the equity of the state aid distribution in the state?" In raising the matter these researchers connect lottery finance with school equity—historically the central subject of school finance research.

Application of ten criterion measures of equity indicates that Florida school spending actually became less equitable in the year after the lottery was enacted. This finding confirms the initial observation that the lottery did not enhance the amounts of money actually spent.

A conceptual model for the net impact of state lottery receipts was developed by Clotfelter and Cook (1989). These economists suggest that lotteries are likely to have a negligible effect on state revenues overall. If winnings are taxed, lotteries may generate a slight increase to the treasury. If they are not, a net loss will occur due to declines in other state tax receipts.

All these investigations are central to the present work. While the studies involve only a few states, taken together they strongly suggest that the lottery movement does not enhance educational spending nationally. At least those who support lotteries as a mechanism for school fiscal enhancement can take no encouragement from the results reported here.

Arguably, however, these are only cases and cases may be atypical. Breadth of coverage did motivate the fifty-state design reported in this book. But a more substantial limitation to the case approach lies deeply embedded in the research design itself. The technique involves comparison of a real set of circumstances with a hypothetical set: what a state *actually did* spend versus an estimate of what the state *would have* spent, if it had not enacted a lottery.

A plethora of rival events besides lotteries may influence calculation of a state's hypothetical educational spending level. Of particular importance here are changes in pupil populations, gross tax receipts, tax reform movements, tax caps, legislative membership, and general state economic conditions. All these contingencies, and others, are known to play a role in the determination of pupil expenditures.

Arguing perversely, one might expect lottery enactment to be associated with a downturn in educational spending, if enactment of this "last resort" revenue measure can only occur in a climate of extreme fiscal stress. Lotteries cannot, any more than other tax enactments, insure the fiscal health of states and communities which school funding requires. Nor can they insure that residents will have favorable attitudes toward public spending.

In this section we reviewed four studies that directly address the relationship between state lotteries and support for public elementary and secondary schools. All cited some evidence of fungibility or the substitution of lottery revenue for more traditional sources of education funding. None claimed that lotteries enhance education funding in any sizeable proportion.

THE PRESENT STUDY

Case studies of individual states have examined trends in support for education before and after the implementation of the lottery. The approach has much to recommend it, but it cannot identify with certainty the influence of lotteries on a state's school finances. We need to find out not only *that* budgets go up, but *why* they go up.

The *why* question is vital because education budgets go up in every state nearly every year. This is true in states which have never operated lotteries, in states which have operated them for many years, and in states implementing lotteries for the first time. Because budgets grow inexorably, the relevant question must be stated, "Do budgets go up *more* after a lottery is implemented than they would have otherwise?"

If, after implementation of a lottery, educational finance trends are adverse, general economic conditions may be blamed. If—contrary to the research findings—finances in a particular state should improve, credit might plausibly be given to a governor, a state legislature, or an improved economy, but not the lottery. Proponents can always claim that the *lottery* money went to education. It was *other* revenues that were lost. Lottery opponents can claim that lottery implementation *causes* other funding to drop. The electorate thinks gambling will take care of the education finance problem and withdraws other sources of support (Shapiro, 1988). This is a conundrum.

In sum, while before/after designs enable one to describe the link between the lottery and public school finance within a particular state, they cannot offer any *explanations as to why* states spend what they do. Furthermore, they do not deal with the lottery-education connection as prevalent, nationwide fiscal policy.

Rather than employing a "before the lottery/after the lottery" design, this study takes a more general approach by attempting to describe and analyze the aggregate fiscal impact of this national phenomenon in financing schools across the country. The year selected was 1987—a year in which a majority of the population, but not yet a majority of the states, had adopted some form of lottery.

The study is grounded within the framework of a political claim postulated by lottery advocates, that the existence of the games correlates positively with educational funding. Claims for and against this view abound, and it is reasonable to assume that this political claim impacts policy (e.g., Hancock, 1987; Hartwig, 1987; Thomas and Webb, 1984). The societal expectation, fostered by proponents that lotteries improve education support, is often a precursor to state lottery adoption, or the addition of new games. Implicit in the claim that lotteries help schools, is the view that states which adopt lotteries are apt to increase fiscal provisions for public education above and beyond what they would have been otherwise. And, by 1987, political and fiscal policy links between lotteries and education had been established in twenty-two states and Washington, D.C. (LaFleur, 1988b).

Two important questions, central to the understanding of the role of lotteries in school finance, can be stated as follows.

(1) To what extent can state lotteries explain variation in support for public education among the states?

(2) Do states which argue that the lottery increases education spending provide greater fiscal support or make greater efforts to fund public schools than (a) states which do not operate lotteries, or (b) states which use lottery revenues for purposes other than public education?

Indicators of Effort and Support for Education

In this study, we refer to four different specific measures, two indicating "support for education" and two indicating "effort for education." Together these four measures, which in composite we call *indicators of support and effort for education* (ISEE), introduce the list of measures in the study.

Per pupil state aid (SA) is the first support variable. SA represents the amount of money allocated for elementary and secondary education

(K–12) in the relevant year, 1987. This measure is key, for if lotteries make a difference then we would logically expect state school aid to be greater in lottery states than in non-lottery states.

Some studies have shown that state aid has a stimulative effect on spending. More state aid encourages local education authorities to tax and spend in greater magnitudes, and indeed this is the principle guiding many of the aid formulas used in the fifty states. Other research suggests the opposite. State aid increases may simply replace local property tax revenues, causing little or no spending change in the aggregate. It is by no means clear, therefore, whether increments in state school aid actually will filter down to the schools themselves (Renshaw, 1960; Bahl and Sanders, 1966; Sacks and Harris, 1964; Ryan, 1985).

The second support variable, *per pupil state-local expenditures* (SL), reflects this ambiguity. Excluding federal funds, this measure tells us whether lottery funds show up on the bottom line, In conjunction with SA, the SL measure will tell us whether lottery aid substitutes for or stimulates spending overall.

Effort for education is a measure of particular interest to educators and specialists in public finance. Effort indices look beyond absolute dollar amounts to measure the tax capacity or "tax paying ability" of state residents. The concept of effort is closely related to the idea of "educational need."

Effort measures assume that it is not simply the raw dollars spent which matter, it is what one spends in relation to what one has. A low income jurisdiction might exert more effort to spend than a high income one, even though the dollars are higher in the latter. The low income jurisdiction is considered more deserving of financial aid, and so effort measures are integral components of state and federal aid formulas, determining the magnitudes of funds flowing to local schools (Advisory Commission on Intergovernmental Relations, 1989; Sparkman, 1977; Sergi, 1977).

The two measures of effort for education used in this study are *state school aid as a percent of state government expenditures* (SAEF1) and *state-local school expenditures as a percent of state personal income* (SLEF2). Taking the second measure first, the SLEF2 statistic adjusts for income and cost of living variations among the states. The statistic goes beyond how raw dollars are spent, to the proportion of total income supporting a particular spending level.

If lottery proponents are correct that lotteries increase school funding, then SLEF2 – effort to spend – should be larger in lottery states. And this should be true regardless of the absolute dollar amounts spent. The reasoning is as follows. In addition to the traditional sales, income, and property taxes, residents pay an additional "voluntary" lottery tax, thus increasing their total income share devoted to schools. One would expect, *a priori,* that effort to spend, as measured by SLEF2, would be higher in lottery states.

SAEF1 provides a measure of the relative priority of schooling in the state's overall budget. The measure is computed by dividing the total amount of state school aid by total state government general expenditures. Other things being equal, one might expect states earmarking lottery funds for education to spend more of their revenues for schools than other states. Again this measure is not directly affected by economic development, because wealthy, urban, industrial states simply spend more for all public functions. These four variables are treated as dependent variables in the model.

The Lottery Variable

This study considers lotteries as political variables; state legislatures determine whether or not to utilize the revenue instrument. This consideration has implications for the treatment of lotteries in the statistical design explained below.

The types of lottery variables employed in this study are twofold. Because of the fungibility of lottery revenues, a question arises about the statutory importance of earmarking. It seems possible that the existence of any lottery, even one not specifically directed to school funding, might enhance school revenues. It was decided therefore to include a statistical variable (L) simply denoting the *presence or absence of a lottery* in a particular state. Employing such a variable in a mathematical regression equation has an additional explanatory benefit. It will help us determine whether states which have implemented lotteries share similar socioeconomic or demographic characteristics.

The second type of variable in which we are interested is *lotteries for education* (LOTED). This variable directly analyzes the substantive importance of statutes using lottery revenue for schools.

All states are categorized into two groups, those with earmarking statutes, and those without them. For this second purpose, states whose lotteries are mainly used to fund other public functions are grouped with states that do not sponsor lotteries. The first variable addresses the question, "Does having a lottery matter for school funding?" The second variable addresses the question, "Does 'earmarking' enhance school revenues?"

The Other Independent Variables

Previous research has identified a large number of variables that can predict school spending levels across the fifty states. Selection of variables is a somewhat subjective matter; there are no absolutely clear theoretical guides. Making the same point with slightly different words, one can say that many social, political, economic, and demographic variables can predict school spending. The rationale for the ones selected here is discussed in more detail in Appendix A. Here it may simply be noted that the seven variables selected commonly serve as proxies for the much larger number of factors affecting education spending (Fabricant, 1952; Bahl, 1969; Barro, 1972; Brazer, 1959; Dye and Gray, 1980; Hickrod, 1971; McMahon, 1970; Rossmiller, 1968).

Among the most influential variables determining a state's level of school spending is the *per capita personal income* (PCI) of its residents. The economic variable PCI is an aggregate of total state income received by persons residing in a state divided by the total state population.

Numerous studies have shown this variable to be an excellent gauge of the ability and willingness of states to generate funds for schools. It runs in the intuitively expected direction. High income states spend more per capita, on average, for their children's education than low income states. Since high income states are expected to spend more, the effects of state income should be minimized or eliminated when considering the question, "Does the lottery help schools?" It is only by controlling for income that we can estimate the unique and independent effect of lotteries.

To minimize theoretical deficiencies, it is important to explain how specific independent variables may be expected to influence expenditure patterns. Since per capita income (PCI) has consistently been one of the most important determinants of public expenditure, it is hypothesized that the correlation coefficient for this variable will be significantly greater than zero. As a measure of wealth, income levels reflect the relative ability of states to fund education.

As a measure of the relative educational load, the *percent of the population which is of school age* (SAP) is an econmic variable directly measuring the fiscal burdens of public education. Conceivably, one might expect "young" states to exhibit different fiscal characteristics and propensities than "old" ones. On the other hand, states with large proportions of public school parents might be willing to tax themselves at higher rates to support the schools. This variable was expected to have a significant and negative relationship with school expenditures. However, based on the literature, the percent of population which is of school age was expected to have a positive correlation with indicators of educational effort.

It was hypothesized that the *percent of the state's population which is non-white* (PNWT) and the *percentage of the population which has completed at least high school* (PPHS) variables affect taste and demand for education. It is well established that race affects social conditions and the labor market. Race is a variable of interest in many sociological studies and may conceivably affect lottery status. The school restructuring movement, for example, has directed special emphasis at inner-city schools which are often primarily African-American or Hispanic. Race has also been a factor in the school finance reform movement.

With regard to educational levels, adults who have experienced more formal schooling themselves are more supportive of it. They are willing to devote higher proportions of their income to education, and the well educated have higher incomes and hence more money to spend on all goods and services, including education. It is assumed that states with a higher proportion of non-whites, illiterates, or people with less than twelve years of schooling, will be associated with low levels of education spending.

Population per square mile (PSQM) and *percent of urban population* (URB) have been found to be significant determinants of school spending (e.g., Fabricant, 1952; Fisher, 1961; Ohls and Wales, 1972; Ryan, 1985; Strudwick, 1985). Researchers have explained this relationship between density and education expenditures with the possible effects of economies of scale. In this study it was hypothesized that higher population density would be generally associated with a reduction in per pupil costs.

Private school enrollment (PVSE) is a social variable that theoretically could influence effort and support for school spending in either direction, up or down. Private school enrollments take a load off of the public schools. Governments have fewer pupils to educate. On the other hand, private school parents are possibly less likely to support public schools. See Appendix A for a more complete discussion of the research on these variables.

Research Design

This research employed a correlational *ex post facto* design. Multiple regression was used to obtain a current estimate of the amount of variance in state indicators of support and effort for education (ISEE), which could be explained by classic socioeconomic and demographic determinants. The selection of predictor variables rested on previous research (e.g., Fabricant, 1952; Shapiro, 1962; Sparkman, 1977; Strudwick, 1985) and *a priori* considerations.

Hierarchical regression was employed to determine the extent to which variance in ISEE could be explained by state lotteries after the effects of the traditional predictors had been taken into account.

The second major question was answered using *t*-tests. "Do states which claim that the lottery enhances school funding actually demonstrate greater support or effort for public schools than states which do not make such a claim?"

Finally, multiple regression procedures were run to determine whether or not the status of states, with regard to a lottery, was related to the same set of determinants that accounted for interstate differences in support and effort for public elementary-secondary education. One of these regression equations was used to determine the extent to which socioeconomic variables from the determinants model could explain whether or not a state used a lottery to support public education (LOTED) in 1987. A second stepwise multiple regression procedure was executed to analyze the relationship between the same socioeconomic and demographic determinants, and the status of states as having operated a lottery in 1987 or not (L). Thus, in both cases the dependent variable takes the form of a discrete dichotomy. The LOTED (lottery for education) variable classifies states according to whether or not they operated lotteries which were purported to enhance funding for public education K–12. The L (lottery) variable simply defines all states and the District of Columbia according to whether or not they operated a lottery in 1987.

The Determinants Model

Based on an extensive review, there is no consensus on one best expenditure determinants model. Many determinants designs have failed to outline hypotheses to support the use of specific independent or predictor variables. Other models had inherent specification errors and were compromised by multicollinearity or autocorrelation difficulties. The model used in this study, adapted extensively from Strudwick (1985) and Barro (1972), attempted to minimize the theoretical and methodological limitations evident in previous determinants research.

Basic theoretical assumptions provide a conceptual framework, and guide the understanding of how this model relates education spending to selected independent variables. The model relies upon the basic economic concepts of "constrained optimization" and public choice theory (Strudwick, 1985). An explanation of these theoretical assumptions is provided below.

Each jurisdiction is viewed as a composite of individuals who exhibit private preferences and motivational characteristics. Individual voters weigh the costs and benefits of a given tax rate, and vote according to individual utility. In simple terms, consumers vote according to their perceptions of how certain laws, policies, and tax rates affect their own needs and wants.

The operational model used here emphasizes the decision-making role of elected and appointed government officials. The link between legislators and voters is seen as being "tenuous and complex." Just as individuals vote to maximize their individual utility, politicians make decisions to maximize their chances of attaining or retaining office. According to this paradigm, promotion of the common good may not be the prime force behind the decisions of legislators. Politicians make decisions that maximize their possibility of election victory. Thus, states' expenditure decisions or public service provisions are seen as outcomes of decision-makers' "efforts to maximize their own utility, which is represented by the probability of reelection" (Strudwick, 1985). This theoretical focus is different from other collective choice theories in that public spending policy is predominantly a function of the political process.

Under these assumptions, each state is treated as a single decision-making unit whose expenditure levels are determined by government officials in charge. The likelihood that the political system will raise taxes to increase education expenditures declines as taxes increase or as income decreases. The general formula is expressed:

$$u = u[\text{PPE}, b(\text{PCI}, t) Z]$$

where,

u = utility function of decision-making unit
PPE = per pupil education expenditure
b = burden function of decision-making unit
PCI = per capita income
t = education taxes
Z = a set of jurisdiction sociodemographic characteristics that affect cost, supply, and preference for education

Per pupil educational expenditure (PPE), a measure of educational output, has an overall positive utility to the jurisdiction. The burden of education taxes (b), a function of income (PCI) and tax per capita (t), has negative utility. A set of sociodemographic characteristics (Z) affects cost and supply and preference levels of educational services and expenditures.

Using econometric theory and mathematical transformations, the theoretical formula can be expressed in a multiple regression form (Strudwick, 1985). The following regression equation incorporates Strudwick's predictor variables with the criterion measures chosen for analysis in this research.

$$\text{ISEE} = \text{PCI} + \text{SAP} + \text{PNWT} + \text{URB}$$

$$+ \text{PSQM} + \text{PPHS} + \text{PVSE} + a$$

where,

ISEE = indicators of support and effort for education. Equations were developed for each of the following indicators (dependent variables):
    SL = per pupil state-local expenditure
    SA = per pupil state aid

SAEF1 = per pupil state aid as a percent of state government expenditures

SLEF2 = per pupil state-local expenditures as a percent of state personal income

PCI = state per capita income in fiscal year 1987

SAP = percent of population that is school age (five to seventeen)

PNWT = percent of state population that is non-white

URB = percent of population living in urban areas

PSQM = population density (persons/square mile)

PPHS = schooling background (percent of population that completed high school)

PVSE = percent of school age population enrolled in non-public schools

a = the regression constant

It is well accepted that some determinants studies lack a strong conceptual base. Research has been criticized for its failure to specify theoretical models and hypotheses. The literature indicates a pressing need to develop such theoretical bases prior to manipulation and interpretation of data. Nevertheless, the case for using an expenditure determinants model was compelling (see Appendix A).

Strudwick's work is invoked here for two major reasons. First, it is the most recent, comprehensive determinants study that uses the state as the unit of analysis. Also, the emphasis on the political process seems particularly applicable to lotteries. Legislators do, in fact, institute lotteries to fund education and other functions, primarily because of budgetary shortfalls within the existing tax structure.

Two different lottery variables were employed. To determine the importance of the lottery as a determinant of educational support and effort, states were categorized according to whether or not their lotteries were purported to enhance education funding. States which earmarked all lottery revenues for education were coded "1" on the LOTED variable. States which claimed that the lottery assisted educational funding, through the flow of revenues through the general fund, were also assigned a value of "1" for the LOTED variable. LOTED was coded "2" for states which, (a) did not operate a lottery in 1987, or (b) made no claims that the lottery improved educational funding K–12. The identical grouping scheme was used in the t-test procedures discussed in Chapter 5.

Data Collection

The data were obtained for the four dependent variables indicating educational effort and support, and the eight independent variables, for fifty states and the District of Columbia. Data cover only one point in time, fiscal year 1987. The year 1987 is one of the last in which there was a roughly even division between lottery and non-lottery states. The figures for other variables are from the U.S. Department of Education, or the U.S. Bureau of the Census and—as closely as possible—applicable to that year. Typically, census data is several years behind finance data.

Since the census is conducted at ten-year intervals, current government documents contain statistics that are actually several years old. The researcher's alternatives are limited in this regard. It has been suggested, however, that a time lag is beneficial in that it takes a period of years for changes in socioeconomic conditions to affect state spending levels or demand for public services (Sergi, 1977; Strudwick, 1985).

In all cases, the data reflected state averages or totals. Data were entered directly into a computer file. All individual and descriptive statistics were checked for possible data entry errors. Since data were collected for all fifty states and the District of Columbia, the universe is the sample.

Data used in the study were gathered from individual state lottery reports, the Public Gaming Research Institute, the Advisory Commission on Intergovernmental Relations, the U.S. Department of Education, the National Education Association, and the U.S. Bureau of the Census.

Objectives and Research Questions

This study has two major objectives.

- Determine the relative importance of state lotteries in the financing of elementary and secondary education in America.
- Determine whether states which claim that the lottery enhances support for education, provide greater dollar amounts or make greater effort for elementary and secondary education than non-lottery states.

These objectives are investigated through four specific research questions.

(1) To what extent and in what manner can four indicators of support and effort for public education K–12 (ISEE) be explained by selected state socioeconomic and demographic variables? This question establishes a timely base of determinants to which lotteries may be compared.

(2) After adjusting for the effects of the significant determinants (in question 1), to what extent can ISEE be explained by states' use of lottery revenues for public education (LOTED)?

(3) Is there any significant difference between states that use lottery funds to support public education K–12, and states that do not, with respect to indicators of support and effort for education (ISEE)?

(4) To what extent can socioeconomic and demographic determinants of ISEE predict the lottery status of states?

Together these four questions provide a basis for evaluating the significance of lotteries in financing the nation's public schools. Answering these questions enables us to determine the relative importance of a variety of factors—those relating directly to a lottery and those that do not—in explaining why states vary among themselves in their total school costs.

Limitations

There are three simplifying assumptions inherent in the specification of this research design. First, it is assumed that educational expenditure figures for fiscal year 1987 reflect lottery revenues collected that same year. Secondly, it is assumed that revenues are derived solely from jurisdictional sources. The possible stimulative or fungible effects of federal aid on state or local educational spending are not addressed by this model. Lastly, this study is cross-sectional in nature. Findings for the year 1987 may not be applicable for other years.

This study is limited to a select group of socioeconomic and demographic variables which, according to the literature, are related to differences in educational funding among governmental units (e.g., Fabricant, Miner, Ryan, Sparkman, Strudwick, Ziegler, and others). Many other variables could have been selected. Reasons for selecting these specific ones are discussed in the appendices.

Factors beyond the scope of this study may be important determinants of support for education, and may be significantly related to the lottery status of individual states. Extraneous variables such as political climate and party affiliation are always threats to validity in studies of this type. What can be said is that the study's design reflects lotteries adopted over a twenty-three year time span in a wide variety of educational policy climates. Since non-lottery states are studied too, and since they were actually the more numerous in 1987, they may be viewed as a sort of control.

In correlation studies the relationships between the explanatory and dependent variables cannot be interpreted as causal. Errors may result because the research inherently lacks the type of controls present in truly experimental designs.

While it may be interesting to use these jurisdictional characteristics to predict those states that are likely to adopt a lottery or extend its present repertoire of games, such an exercise is beyond the scope of the research design.

CONCLUSION

Two questions are central to this study. The first question is "Do lottery states spend more for education that non-lottery states?" This is addressed by grouping states according to lottery status and examining their levels of educational support. Standard and widely accepted indices of educational support have been developed to facilitate comparisons. These indices are applied to groups of lottery and non-lottery states.

The second question is "How important are lotteries in explaining interstate variation in support for education?" This is actually the more relevant and interesting one. We know from any tabulation of school spending across the fifty states that some of them will spend more than others. Some states are larger, or richer, or have higher percentages of school age children than others. Some states have income and sales taxes while others do not, and so on. These variables, among many others, will affect spending.

The task, then, is to isolate the distinct effects of a lottery from the myriad of other factors affecting spending. Fortunately there are established procedures to help address this task. Political scientists, economists, and researchers from other disciplines have developed theories that account for variations in state-local spending levels. Called "expenditure determinants studies," school finance researchers have used the results of these research efforts to explain why governments choose particular levels of education spending.

The expenditure determinants approach assumes there are relevant background factors, common among the states, that can be used to explain variations in their spending patterns. The background factors that researchers may employ vary from study to study, but the variables are economic, social, demographic, and/or political in nature.

Prior determinants studies have successfully explained and predicted state-local spending on education specifically. A substantial body of knowledge exists to account for inequities in fiscal provisions and the relative spending efforts among cities, states, and school districts. The numerous investigations that have been done explain approximately 20 to 80 percent of the variance in school spending. The present study relies substantially on the successes of these past efforts.

Lotteries are the new variable, used as an expenditure determinant here for the first time. If lotteries can account for interstate variations in school spending and tax effort, there are two effects. At the practical level, the model can determine whether lotteries do, in fact, enhance educational funding as their proponents claim. At the conceptual level, specialist researchers can better understand those factors that determine state fiscal behavior.

CHAPTER 5

Do Lotteries Enhance School Support?

IN 1987, eighteen states reported that their lotteries contributed to the financing of public schools. It follows that these states which use lotteries to enhance school funding should demonstrate higher levels of support and effort than states which use lottery revenues for other purposes or states which do not operate lotteries at all. Such findings would have significant implications for educators, state policy analysts, and industry advocates.

THE STATUS OF STATE LOTTERIES IN 1987

By 1987, twenty-two states and the District of Columbia had lotteries and twenty-eight states still did not. All states in the Northeast had adopted lotteries. Eleven jurisdictions assigned the revenue to the general fund for allocation at the discretion of the state legislature, or used the funds for revenue sharing to cities and towns. Five states allocated lottery profits for public projects such as transportation, conservation, economic development, and senior citizens' programs. The remaining seven states earmarked all or a major portion of their revenues to public schools (see Table 5.1).

In 1987, most non-lottery states were located in the South or in the sparsely populated sections of the West (see Figure 3.1). All of the very large states except Florida and Texas had lotteries. But several of the middle-sized and more affluent northern states, notably Wisconsin, Minnesota, and Indiana, were non-lottery states at that time. Approx-

Table 5.1. Profile of State Lotteries, 1987.

State	Initial Operation	Lottery Revenues 1987 (millions)	Per Capita Sales 1987	Primary use of Revenue
Arizona	1981	$ 142	$ 41.99	Local Transportation
California	1985	$ 1,400	$ 50.33	Public Education
Colorado	1983	$ 116	$ 34.37	Capital Construction, Conservation, Parks and Recreation
Connecticut	1972	$ 489	$152.38	General Fund
Delaware	1975	$ 46	$ 71.10	General Fund
District of Columbia	1982	$ 123	$195.68	General Fund
Illinois	1974	$ 1,300	$112.58	Public Education
Iowa	1985	$ 95	$ 33.35	Economic Development, Agriculture, Education
Maine	1974	$ 58	$ 48.93	General Fund
Maryland	1973	$ 761	$167.70	General Fund
Massachusetts	1972	$ 1,500	$215.16	Revenue Sharing to Cities and Towns, Arts
Michigan	1972	$ 1,000	$109.38	Public Education
Missouri	1986	$ 180	$ 34.17	General Fund
New Hampshire	1964	$ 59	$ 56.97	Public Education
New Jersey	1971	$ 1,100	$145.59	Public Education, State Institutions, $75,000 to Compulsive Gambling Studies
New York	1976	$ 1,500	$ 81.84	Public Education
Ohio	1974	$ 1,100	$ 99.21	Public Education
Oregon	1985	$ 101	$ 36.83	Economic Development
Pennsylvania	1972	$ 1,300	$112.14	Senior Citizens
Rhode Island	1974	$ 59	$ 58.74	General Fund
Vermont	1978	$ 25	$ 46.21	General Fund
Washington	1982	$ 194	$ 42.74	General Fund
West Virginia	1985	$ 68	$ 37.22	General Fund
Total		$12,716	$ 86.29	

Data from LaFleur (1988a). Use of revenue figures from U.S. Bureau of the Census (1988a).

imately two-thirds of the population lived in states which had legalized games, but lotteries were still illegal in the majority of states (U.S. Bureau of the Census, 1988b). Thus for 1987 we can reasonably assume that the two groups of states — lottery and non-lottery — were fairly similar in their range of measures of socioeconomic and demographic variables used in this study. This assumption is important in assessing the validity of our comparisons (Kerlinger, 1986). The assumption would be more questionable in the early 1980s when fewer states had lotteries, or in the 1990s, when the vast proportion of the population lived in lottery jurisdictions.

From the discussion in Chapter 1 it is clear that the two decades prior to 1987 witnessed an ever-increasing state role in the financing of public services. But that growth was halting and uneven within specific jurisdictions and regions of the country. In the 1970s and early 1980s, inflation, high interest rates, fuel shortages, unemployment, tremors in the stock market, and other fiscal crises frequently reduced a state's tax receipts from traditional revenue sources. Tax revolt measures, such as Propositions 13 in California and 2-1/2 in Massachusetts, hit local governments, including school districts, particularly hard. Such adversities only served to increase demands for public services. In those locales, politicians and policy analysts were driven to search for alternatives to either raising broad-based taxes or instituting new ones, setting the stage for lottery adoption.

The success of this form of public gaming exceeded all projections. The phenomenal growth and popularity of state-sponsored gambling is manifested in lottery revenues, which soared from $1.4 billion in 1977 to $14.8 billion in 1988 (see Table 5.2). After administration costs and prizes, government proceeds totaled $5.6 billion in the latter year. As of 1987, approximately $28 billion had been returned to state coffers since New Hampshire had reintroduced the American lottery more than two decades earlier. The California, New York, and Illinois lotteries each generated more than $2 million per day.

These amounts were by no means insignificant. School revenues generated directly by these earmarked funds equaled approximately 30 percent of the total federal school aid. Of the seven states that earmarked lottery profits for education in 1987, Michigan, Ohio, and New Jersey generated more lottery revenue than they received from the federal government for the same purpose (see Table 5.3). If all states that operated lotteries in 1987 had used the money for elementary-

Table 5.2. Growth of State Lotteries, 1977–1988.

Year	Lottery Revenues (millions)	Government Proceeds (millions)	Number of Lottery States
1977	$ 1,445	$ 578	13
1978	$ 1,820	$ 724	14
1979	$ 2,037	$ 807	14
1980	$ 2,350	$ 961	14
1981	$ 2,880	$ 1,169	15
1982	$ 3,794	$ 1,535	17
1983	$ 5,166	$ 2,072	18
1984	$ 6,736	$ 2,890	18
1985	$ 8,913	$ 3,707	21
1986	$12,200	$ 4,876	23
1987	$12,716	$ 4,931	23
1988	$14,849	$ 5,646	28
Total	$74,906	$29,896	

Data for 1977–1986 from Hancock (1987). Data for 1987 and 1988 from LaFleur (1988a).

secondary education, lottery contributions in nine of these states would have exceeded per pupil federal school aid. Michigan's lottery profits amounted to 23 percent of all revenues in the state's school aid fund during the 1984–1985 fiscal year. Without this support, hypothetically, the average Michigan household would have paid nearly $115 more in taxes to finance education at the same spending levels (Hancock, 1987).

In addition to the money specifically designated for education in these seven "earmark" states, a substantial amount of lottery revenue is channeled to education via the general fund. In their annual reports, states which assigned lottery profits to the general fund implicitly or explicitly purported that the money enhanced educational appropriations.

STATISTICAL PROCEDURES AND RESULTS

Statistical procedures, described here and in the previous chapter, were performed to assess the relationship between state lotteries and interstate variation in four indices of support and effort for education. The simple determinants model uses socioeconomic and demographic indicators from the literature to explain variation in each of the following four measures indicating support and effort for education.

(1) Per pupil state aid (SA)

(2) Per pupil state-local expenditures (SL)

(3) State aid as a percent of state government expenditures (SAEFl)

(4) State-local expenditures as a percent of personal income (SLEF2)

At the next stage, the lottery variable (LOTED) was added to the multiple regression model. The increase in predictive power (R^2) and

Table 5.3. A Comparison of Federal School Aid and State Lottery Revenue in 1987, Expressed in Dollars Per Pupil in Average Daily Attendance.

State	Federal Aid	Lottery Revenues	Government Proceeds
Arizona	344.78	244.60	78.82
California	296.23	415.91	163.17
Colorado	218.64	199.38	57.46
Connecticut	256.97	949.24	380.00
Delaware	416.27	481.74	196.51
District of Columbia	341.75	1,556.30	579.10
Illinois	348.86	800.47	336.75
Iowa	219.35	179.42	60.54
Maine	273.89	195.36	59.72
Maryland	271.36	1,212.48	545.97
Massachusetts	282.46	1,520.06	512.91
Michigan	203.60	674.80	280.24
Missouri	222.68	289.81	289.81
New Hampshire	140.71	227.00	72.83
New Jersey	293.58	961.55	406.15
New York	335.33	578.44	266.19
Ohio	192.52	564.32	222.80
Oregon	292.24	217.79	70.50
Pennsylvania	228.03	850.83	355.91
Rhode Island	194.95	465.84	176.49
Vermont	285.50	142.94	38.92
Washington	253.30	260.18	103.57
West Virginia	523.36	169.37	60.58

Note: federal aid and attendance data from National Education Association (1988). Lottery revenue data from bureau of state lotteries, by individual state.

the significance of each variable (beta) were examined in each of the four equations. If the predictive power of the model increased, lotteries did enhance school spending. If the predictive power did not change, or changed insignificantly, lotteries did not help.

Four statistical tests (*t*-tests) were performed to determine if the two groups of states, lottery versus non-lottery, differed significantly with respect to indicators of support and effort for education. In ancillary analyses, multiple regression was employed to determine the extent to which the socioeconomic and demographic variables from the basic determinants model could predict the lottery status of states.

This chapter presents the results and a discussion of these statistical analyses. It is organized around four general areas of inquiry which underlie the corresponding sets of null hypotheses presented in Chapters 1 and 4. These null hypotheses guide the statistical procedures outlined above.

The Determinants of Interstate Variation in Support and Effort for Education

The data are analyzed to assess the extent to which variance in each indicator of support and effort for public education K–12 is explained by the following set of socioeconomic and demographic variables.

(1) Per capita income (PCI)

(2) School age population (SAP)

(3) Percent of population non-white (PNWT)

(4) Urbanization (URB)

(5) Private school enrollment (PVSE)

(6) Population density (PSQM)

(7) Educational attainment of the population (PPHS)

The determinants model hypothesizes that enduring socioeconomic and demographic characteristics from the literature are good theoretical explainers of interstate variation in support for education. The socioeconomic and demographic characteristics represent the following theoretical influences on demand for education: ability to spend (per capita income), educational load (school age population), cost influences (population density, urbanization), and taste and preference (percent of population non-white, private school enrollment, educational attainment of the population). In addition, given the billions of dollars that lotteries generate for public education and the claims made by lottery proponents, this study considers whether or not state lotteries may also be a significant determinant of interstate variation in support for public schools.

Before presenting regression results, we examine the correlations between the predictor and criterion variables. This allows us to compare the hypothesized relationships from the theoretical model with the observed correlations. Of course, the possible influence of state lotteries is our prime concern. However, an understanding of the explanatory ability of "traditional" determinants of public education spending is a prerequisite for any appreciation of the possible value of state lotteries in financing schools.

Correlations

Table 5.4 contains the correlation coefficients between the four dependent and eight independent variables. The correlations range from a low of − .018 between percent of population non-white (PNWT) and per pupil state-local expenditures (SL), to a high of .784 between per capita income (PCI) and per pupil state-local expenditures.

Per capita income is the measure most widely used in federal grant formulas and elsewhere as an indicator of fiscal capacity (Advisory Commission on Intergovernmental Relations, 1989). Since per capita income is considered to be a measure of ability, it was expected that state per capita income would be significantly and positively correlated

Table 5.4. Pearson Product Moment Correlations between
Independent and Dependent Variables.

Dependent Variables ISEE	Independent Variables							
	PCI	PSQM	URB	PVSE	PNWT	PPHS	SAP	LOTED
SA	.454	.537	−.086	.246	.479	.092	−.263	.188
SL	.784	.273	.239	.387	−.018	.345	−.446	.452
SAEF1	−.209	−.066	.051	−.120	.134	−.191	.125	−.167
SLEF2	−.099	−.178	−.348	−.369	−.316	.389	.416	−.072

Note: coefficients of .246 and greater are significant at the .05 level. Correlations are for all fifty states and the District of Columbia.

with state-local expenditures per pupil. A coefficient of .784 between these two variables reaffirms the overwhelming body of research indicating the strong relationship between school spending and state personal income. The association between per capita income and state aid per pupil (SA) is also positive and significant, although somewhat weaker, than the relationship between per capita income and per pupil state-local expenditures. This suggests that the influence of income remains significant despite the wide range of school aid formulas and interstate disparity in the percentage of school revenues generated at the state level.

The relationship between per capita income and per pupil state aid as a percent of state general expenditures (SAEF1) is negative and insignificant ($r = -.209$). Similarly the relationship between per capita income and state-local expenditures as a percent of state personal income (SLEF2) is very small and insignificant. Since per capita income is considered a measure of ability to finance education, high ability states in general are not necessarily high effort states.

The school age population (SAP) can be considered a measure of educational load and as such was expected to influence the cost of educational provision. If economies of scale are operating, larger loads may be associated with lower unit cost. If ability and effort are held constant, then by definition, higher loads result in lower expenditures per pupil. It was hypothesized that school age population would be significantly and negatively associated with educational spending. As indicated in Table 5.4, school age population is significantly correlated with state aid, per pupil state-local expenditures, and educational effort as a percent of personal income. School age population has negative correlations with the direct spending variables (state aid and per pupil state-local expenditures). Together these findings suggest that states with higher percentages of school age residents spend less per pupil in state aid and combined state-local expenditures. Also, states with greater educational loads seem to exert more spending effort.

Population density (PSQM) has a moderately positive correlation with state aid and a lower, but nevertheless significant, positive correlation with per pupil state-local expenditures. Rather than operating economies or diseconomies of scale, it may be that citizens in more densely populated states want higher levels of education provision and pay more for it. The correlations between population density and both measures of tax effort to finance education are negative but insignificant.

It was expected that higher urban costs would result in positive correlations between the urbanization variable (URB) and direct spending indicators. However, as indicated in Table 5.4, urbanization has an insignificant correlation with state aid and a positive, significant correlation with per pupil state-local expenditures. Urbanization is significantly and negatively correlated with SLEF2 ($r = -.348$). This association may suggest that residents in more urban states spend less of their income on education. Urban residents simply demand more services, leaving fewer financial resources for public education.

The expected direction of the relationship between private school enrollment (PVSE) and school spending was questionable. Large percentages of private school enrollment can be interpreted as a state's taste for "good" education. Under this assumption we would expect a positive relationship between school spending and private school enrollment. This relationship could also be explained by decreased load on public school systems. Table 5.4 indicates that private school enrollment is significantly associated with state aid, per pupil state-local expenditures, and (negatively) with school spending, expressed as a percentage of personal income. State aid and per pupil state-local expenditures have positive coefficients with private school enrollment suggesting resident preferences for "quality" education or indicating decreased loads on public schools.

The former hypothesis seems to be compromised by the negative relationships between private school enrollment and the second effort measure, state-local expenditures as a percent of state personal income. A preference for good or expensive education seems incompatible with reduced effort. The significant inverse relationship between private school enrollment and effort for education is possibly a function of the moderately high correlation (.498) between private school enrollment and per capita income (see Table 5.5). It appears that high income states are more likely to use private schools, but spend a lower percentage of income on public schools. Since private schools are, on average, less expensive than public ones, people may feel that public school costs should be brought down to a lower level.

States with high percentages of non-white residents (PNWT) were expected to demonstrate lower per pupil spending levels. However, Table 5.4 shows that the percent of population which is non-white has a moderate positive correlation with state aid. The relationship between percent of population non-white and per pupil state-local expenditures is insignificant. Percent of population non-white has a negative

Table 5.5. Pearson Product Moment Correlations among Independent Variables.

	PCI	PSQM	URB	PVSE	PNWT	PPHS	SAP
PSQM	.422						
URB	.475	−.227					
PVSE	.498	.337	.384				
PNWT	.192	.565	.000	.332			
PPHS	.172	.013	−.124	−.096	−.238		
SAP	−.670	−.484	−.309	−.509	−.217	.099	
LOTED	−.526	.266	.265	.433	−.026	−.096	.422

Note: coefficients of .238 and greater are significant at the .05 level.

significant relationship with a state's personal income share devoted to schools (SLEF2). These findings, taken together, suggest that non-whites are today perhaps concentrated in wealthier states rather than in the poorer areas of the deep South.

The educational attainment of the population [percentage of residents who completed high school (PPHS)] is considered to be another variable that may reflect taste or preference for education. It was hypothesized that higher levels of educational attainment of the population would indicate increased demand for public education, but the relationship between state aid and educational attainment of the population proved to be insignificant. In contrast, the association between per pupil state-local expenditures and educational attainment of the population is significantly positive ($r = .345$). The coefficients between educational attainment of the population and each measure of effort have opposite signs. A correlation coefficient of .389 ($p < .05$) between the second effort measure and educational attainment of the population indicates that state-local expenditures as a percent of personal income are higher in states with larger percentages of residents with twelve or more years of schooling. These states seem to spend more of their income on public schools. Since high school completion rates are relatively high, perhaps future studies would have more success using college statistics.

Most lottery states claim that the games enhance support for public schools. It was expected that the lottery status of the states (LOTED) would have positive correlation coefficients with indicators of support.

It is important to note that there is no previous research upon which to base this hypothesis. As discussed previously, this expectation is based on the fact that states sometimes adopt lottery legislation with the expectation that certain state provisions will receive new or improved support. Seventeen states and the District of Columbia reported that their lotteries helped to support public schools in 1987.

There is a significant, positive correlation ($r = .446$) between the lottery status of states and per pupil state-local expenditures. The correlations between LOTED and the other three measures are insignificant. Thus, based on these simple correlations, it appears that state-local per pupil expenditures are generally higher in states which claim that their lotteries help to finance public schools. Hence, there is some evidence that states which claimed that their lotteries enhanced education funding in 1987 actually demonstrated higher state-local spending.

Table 5.5 presents intercorrelations among the independent variables. An examination of these coefficients increases understanding of the link between state environmental characteristics, lottery status, and support and effort for education. The simple r of $-.543$ between lottery status of the states and per capita income indicates that "lottery for education" states have significantly higher levels of per capita income. A correlation coefficient of .422 between school age population and lottery status of the states suggests that states which do not use a lottery to help finance schools also have higher percentages of students ages five to seventeen than higher income states that operate lotteries. In addition, an inspection of Table 5.5 reveals that states which use lottery revenues to enhance elementary and secondary school funding are more densely populated, and have higher private school enrollments.

Based on Table 5.5 several other generalizations can also be made. First, higher income states are more densely populated, have higher private school enrollments, and have smaller percentages of school age children. Also, states with higher percentages of students enrolled in private schools have lower proportions of students aged five to seventeen.

Multiple Regression Analyses

Tables 5.6–5.9 depict the results of the stepwise regression procedures developed from the basic determinants model presented in the last chapter. Different combinations of independent variables explain between 3 percent and 67 percent of the variance in the support and ef-

Table 5.6. Stepwise Multiple Regression and Multiple Correlation Coefficients of the Basic Determinants Model Explaining Variation in Per Pupil State Aid (SA) (N = 51).

Step Number	Variable Entered	R	R^2	SE Est.	Increase in R^2	Beta	t
1	PCI	.593	.351	706.8	NA	.553	3.756*
2	PNWT	.645	.403	685.1	.052	.372	3.298**
3	URB	.676	.457	660.4	.005	.346	2.786**
4	LOTED	.675	.457	660.7	.000	−.012	0.089

*$p < .001$.
**$p < .01$.
Note: variables above the dotted line are significant predictors.

Table 5.7. Stepwise Multiple Regression and Multiple Correlation Coefficients of the Basic Determinants Model Explaining Variation in Per Pupil State-Local Expenditures (SL) (N = 51).

Step Number	Variable Entered	R	R^2	SE Est.	Increase in R^2	Beta	t
1	PCI	.784	.614	672.7	NA	.696	6.659*
2	PPHS	.812	.659	638.5	.045	.234	2.651**
3	LOTED	.815	.665	638.5	.006	.088	0.852

*$p < .001$.
**$p < .05$.
Note: variables above the dotted line are significant predictors.

Table 5.8. Stepwise Multiple Regression and Multiple Correlation Coefficients of the Basic Determinants Model Explaining Variation in State Aid as Percent of State General Expenditures (SAEFl) (N = 51).

Step Number	Variable Entered	R	R^2	SE Est.	Increase in R^2	Beta	t
1	LOTED	.166	.027	.235	NA	.166	1.183

Note: variable is not a significant predictor.

Table 5.9. Stepwise Multiple Regression and Multiple Correlation
Coefficients of the Basic Determinants Model Explaining Variation
in State-Local Education Expenditures as a Percent of
State Personal Income (SLEF2) (N = 51).

Step Number	Variable Entered	R	R²	SE Est.	Increase in R²	Beta	t
1	SAP	.416	.173	7.58	NA	.444	3.329*
2	PPHS	.544	.296	7.07	.123	.360	2.961*
3	LOTED	.560	.315	7.05	.019	.151	1.129

*$p < .01$.
Note: variables above the dotted line are significant predictors.

fort indicators. Each optimal equation contains a different combination of predictors.

These four tables present the results of hierarchical regression procedures that are used to determine the relative ability of a state's lottery status to predict interstate variations in indicators of support and effort for education. Discussion of the hierarchical regression is reserved for the next section of this chapter.

The first stepwise procedure is designed to determine the extent to which interstate variations in state aid could be explained by per capita income, school age population, urbanization, non-white percent of population, private school enrollment, education attainment of the population, and population density. Table 5.6 indicates that when these variables were entered in a stepwise method, per capita income entered the regression equation first. At this step the multiple correlation of .593 equates to a coefficient of determination of .351. At the second step in the equation, non-white percent of population enters and raises the amount of explained variation to about 40 percent. Urbanization enters at the third step and together these three predictors explain 46 percent of the variance in state aid. Since the other variables cannot add predictive power to the equation, they do not enter into the stepwise procedure.

Given the simple r of .784 between per capita income and per pupil state-local expenditures, it might be expected that per capita income would be the best predictor of state-local expenditures. This variable alone explains approximately 61 percent of the variation in per pupil state-local dollars spent, suggesting that, overwhelmingly, it is high income states that spend more on their public schools. Educational attainment of the population is the second and only other significant predictor in this stepwise procedure. Together, per capita income and educational attainment of the population explain 66 percent of the variation in per pupil state-local expenditures (Table 5.7).

Sparkman (1977) and other researchers have been able to explain considerably smaller portions of variance in effort for education than variance in actual per pupil spending. This study is no exception. Table 5.8 shows that none of the independent variables entered in a stepwise method. In this study no social, economic, demographic, or political variables influenced the proportion of their budgets states devote to education. In balancing the needs of education with other social services, education fares about equally well regardless of states' income levels, racial or social composition.

In the stepwise procedure with state-local spending effort as the dependent variable, school age population enters the equation first and explains 17 percent of the variation in this effort index. The entrance of educational attainment of the population at step 2 increases the R^2 value to .30 (see Table 5.9). Again, no other variables, including the lottery variable, are significant predictors.

An Analysis of State Lotteries as a Determinant of Support and Effort for Education

The central purpose of this study is to determine whether state lotteries explain variations among the states in their support for the public schools. In no equation does the lottery status of a state correlate significantly with support and effort for education.

The first regression procedure explains variation in state aid (see Table 5.6). The lottery for education (LOTED) variable enters on step 4, after per capita income, non-white percent of population, and urbanization. At this step the predictive power of the equation (R^2) does not increase. This leveling off of R^2 is accompanied by a slight increase in the standard error of measurement, clearly indicating the lack of predictive value of the lottery variable. The magnitude and insignificant t value of beta is further testimony to apparent insignificance of the lottery status of the state as a determinant of per pupil state aid.

As indicated in Table 5.7, LOTED is also unable to explain a significant amount of variance in per pupil state-local expenditures. When lottery status of the states is entered into the equation at step 3, R^2 shows a very slight increase from .659 at step 2 to .665. The increase of .006 in R^2 is clearly insignificant. The beta of .088 and its concomitant, nonsignificant t value reaffirm the lack of predictive ability of the lottery status of the states in explaining per pupil state-local expenditures.

An examination of Tables 5.8 and 5.9 reveals that a lottery, which is purported to support public schools, has negligible ability to predict either measure of effort to fund education after the effects of "traditional" predictors have been taken into account. In Table 5.8 the lottery status of the states is unable to explain any significant amount of variance when it is forced into the regression equation.

In Table 5.9 we see that the lottery status of the states is entered into the equation after educational attainment of the population has entered in a stepwise fashion. When lottery status is entered at step 3, the predictive power of the equation increases from .296 to .315. This increase of almost 2 percent in explained variance is the largest change accounted for by the lottery variable in any of the equations. Nevertheless, the influence of lottery status in explaining interstate variation in SLEF2 remains insignificant in relation to the explanatory ability of school age population and educational attainment of the population. An examination of the betas and t values reaffirms this conclusion.

Lottery Status as a Determinant of Support and Effort for Education

After testing the assumption of equal variances, pooled t-tests were conducted to answer the following question: "Is there any significant difference between states that used lottery funds to support public schools K–12 and states that did not with respect to indicators of support and effort for education?" Table 5.10 contains the results of the four t-tests. The fifty states and the District of Columbia have been divided into two distinct groups. Jurisdictions which claimed that the lottery enhanced educational funding in 1987 were "yes" states. States which did not operate a lottery in that year (or claimed to use lottery revenue for another dedicated purpose) were categorized as "no" states.

The two groups of states are listed under each dependent variable. The means, standard deviations, standard errors of estimate, degrees of freedom, and pooled variance t values are also presented in the table. Results of the first t-test indicate that states which earmarked all lottery

Table 5.10. Differences in Indicators of Support and Effort for Education (ISEE) between States Which Use a Lottery to Support Public Schools and States Which Do Not (LOTED).

Variable and Group	Mean	Standard Deviation	SE	df	t Value
SA					
LOTED yes	2,247	995	228		
				49	1.34
LOTED no	1,913	768	135		
SL					
LOTED yes	4,348	970	223		
				49	3.54*
LOTED no	3,362	964	170		
SAEF1					
LOTED yes	.153	.055	.013		
				49	2.42**
LOTED no	.235	.289	.050		
SLEF2					
LOTED yes	.0405	.006	.0015		
				49	0.50
LOTED no	.0417	.009	.0016		

*$p < .01$.
**$p < .05$.

funds for public schools, together with states which channeled lottery funds to cities and towns via the general fund, had a mean per pupil state aid figure of $2,247 in the year 1987. The mean for states that did not operate a lottery and states that ran a lottery but used the funds for another purpose was $1,913. The t value of 1.34 indicates that these two means are not significantly different.

A second t-test determined that the mean in per pupil state-local education expenditures is significantly ($p < .01$) higher in those states which claimed that the lottery helped public schools. The states that claimed to give lottery monies to schools had an average state-local expenditure of $4,348. The other thirty-two states had a mean spending level of $3,362.

Significant mean differences ($p < .05$) in education's state budget share are also indicated by the lottery status of the states. In states where it was claimed that the lottery enhanced public school finance, per pupil state aid averaged 15.3 percent of per pupil state general expenditures. Per pupil state aid in the other states averaged 23.5 percent of state general expenditures.

Citizens in both categories of states spent approximately four cents out of every dollar earned on public education K–12. A *t* value of 0.50 indicates no significant difference between the means of the two groups.

The Determinants of State Lottery Status

States' decisions to hold lotteries are related to their social and economic characteristics. The lottery status of a state serves as a proxy for other social and economic variables. To attempt to quantify this relationship, two stepwise multiple regression procedures were run to determine the extent to which the lottery status of the states can be explained by the set of independent variables from the basic determinants model. The possibility of multicollinearity should always be considered in multiple regression. This additional analysis helps determine the extent of multicollinearity between the lottery status of the states and the socioeconomic and demographic determinants.

Lottery status of the states, a dichotomous variable, was regressed on the seven socioeconomic and demographic variables from our model. With no previous research upon which to base the determination of lottery status of the states, a stepwise procedure was used. Table 5.11 indicates that per capita income was the only significant predictor, explaining a modest 28 percent of the variance in the lottery status of the states. Whether or not a lottery state says that the money goes to schools appears to make no difference, in our analysis. Finally the lottery status of states is analyzed regardless of the claim to support education from the proceeds. Since most lottery states report that the revenues help to support public schools, it was expected that environmental characteristics would be able to explain approximately the same amount of variance in the previous equation. As displayed in Table 5.12, per capita income is the only significant predictor, again ex-

Table 5.11. Stepwise Multiple Regression of LOTED on Socioeconomic and and Demographic Variables from the Determinants Model (N = 51).

Step Number	Variable Entered	R	R²	SE Est.	Beta	t
1	PCI	.526	.277	.419	.526	4.334*

*$p < .001$.

Table 5.12. Stepwise Multiple Regression of L on Socioeconomic and Demographic Variables from the Determinants Model (N = 51).

Step Number	Variable Entered	R	R^2	SE Est.	Beta	t
1	PCI	.521	.271	.433	.521	4.271*

*$p < .001$.

plaining approximately 28 percent of the variance in lottery status of states. Whether states have a lottery or not appears to have no influence on their school funding provisions.

CONCLUSION

The first research question sought those social, economic, demographic, and political variables which best explain states' financial support and effort to fund the public schools. With regard to this question, personal income variations among the states are the best explainer of variations in support for the public schools. The proportion of the population that is non-white and the population density are also related to spending and effort.

State spending efforts are measured by the share of the budget going to public schools and by the share of personal income devoted to them. Using these measures, "effort" is not as well explained as "support" in our models. The proportion of the population that is school age and the proportion of adults with high school degrees or better, are two variables positively associated with education effort.

The other lines of analysis probe the significance of the lottery variable specifically. Underlying these analyses is a model that views lottery revenues as a discrete and independent variable under the control of legislatures. It is legislatures that make the lottery decision; they arise within the context of preexisting social, economic, and demographic conditions within each state. Results of research question two show that once these preexisting conditions are accounted for, the legislative decision to have a lottery doesn't significantly impact interstate variations in effort and support for education.

Research question three treats the lottery/non-lottery states as two distinct groups. Lottery states do spend more. This is because they are wealthier than non-lottery states, not because they have the lottery. Non-lottery states actually devote a larger share of their more limited income to support education. In 1987, non-lottery states tried harder to support education than lottery states did.

A final line of analysis deals expressly with states' claims that lottery revenues go to support education. A state's "lottery-for-education" claim makes no significant difference in its educational provision.

These are the highlights among the findings. We go on to discuss their significance in the next chapter.

CHAPTER 6

A New View

AFTER more than seventy years of national abolition, New Hampshire reintroduced the American lottery in 1964. During the political debate that took place in that state, the lottery was justified because revenues from it would be used to do good works. Specifically, the lottery was viewed as an alternative to the levy of new or increased taxes for education. Since lottery legalization in New Hampshire, education costs have always figured heavily in the political debate. To establish and maintain support for state lottery proposals, politicians and industry advocates continue to cite lottery contributions for popular causes, especially the public schools.

In the three decades since New Hampshire acted, tax revolt measures, school finance equalization, educational reform and restructuring, demands for increased public services, and other fiscal crises have prompted other states to follow. The lottery is now well established as a supplemental means of public finance. Currently, thirty-two American jurisdictions have lotteries. Legalization of video lotteries and efforts to implement still newer versions of the game proceed apace. In thirty years, lottery policies have changed from prohibition to promotion. States are lotteries' major beneficiaries as well as their sole regulators.

Despite their popularity and acceptance, lotteries have many opponents who charge that the games constitute dubious public policy. Academicians, journalists, and others assert that the games are immoral; they are identified with regressive, inefficient taxes and compulsive gambling. Adversaries also argue that lotteries compromise citizen re-

115

spect for government, undermine the work ethic, and prey upon the hopes and dreams of individuals who aren't made fully aware that their chances of winning are infinitesimal.

As of 1987, eighteen states had adopted a policy establishing public education as a major recipient of net lottery revenues. Seven states named schools as the sole recipient of lottery funds. The other eleven routed some lottery monies to education through the general fund, or by designating schools as one among several recipients.

In essence, states justify government-sponsored gambling with the contention that lottery contributions to public schools are an important investment in the common good and outweigh the undetermined economic, political, and social costs. In opposition, some educational policy analysts find that lotteries may have overall negative effects on public school funding (Borg and Mason, 1987, 1990; Stewart, 1987; Stark et al., 1991).

SUMMARY OF FINDINGS

The purpose of this study is to describe and analyze the relationship between state lotteries and interstate variation in support and effort for public education. The primary research model is built upon assumptions of public expenditure theory.

Socioeconomic and demographic variables from the literature were selected to represent cost factors, fiscal ability, and the preferences of residents living in individual states. Using 1987 data, indicators of support and spending effort were regressed on the state characteristics. Hierarchical regression techniques were used to control for the influence of the significant determinants and facilitated examination of the relative ability of lotteries to explain interstate variation in each indicator of support and each measure of effort. *t*-Tests were conducted to establish whether or not those states that support schools with lottery revenues exhibit higher levels of support or effort as measured by the following indices: (1) per pupil state aid, (2) per pupil state-local expenditures, (3) state aid as a percent of state general expenditures, and (4) state-local expenditures as a percent of state personal income. To examine further the relationship between lotteries and school finance policy, the lottery status of states was regressed on the determinants of school effort and spending.

School Support and State Characteristics

Seven socioeconomic and demographic variables were used to predict interstate variation in support and effort for education. Our findings reaffirm the importance of wealth, as measured by per capita income, in determining support for education. Of the variables considered in the model, state per capita income is the most powerful environmental determinant of per pupil state aid and per pupil state-local expenditures.

Per capita income, the percent of population that is non-white, and urbanization together explain approximately 46 percent of the interstate variance in state aid. Per capita state income is also the most important explainer of per pupil state-local expenditures. This variable alone explains about 61 percent of the variation across states in what they spend on schools. Per capita income emerges as the major significant predictor. This is true whether the income variable is considered alone or in combination with other variables. These analyses identify the urbanized states of the Northeast and industrial Midwest as the nation's highest spenders on their public schools.

Discussion in Chapter 4 pointed out that expenditure determinants studies, in general, are far less effective in predicting *effort* for education than what is actually raised or spent. Effort in this study includes two variables: the propostion of personal income spent on schools and the percentage share of state budgets devoted to this purpose. The model proved unsuccessful in predicting school aid as a share of state budgets. School age population together with adults' school completion rates account for 30 percent of the interstate variation in school expenditure as a percent of state personal income. Residents tend to spend a greater percentage of their income on education in states where the school age populations are larger and in states with larger percentages of high school graduates.

In the most general terms, these preliminary analyses confirm the findings of the past generation of school finance research. There are substantial differences among states in their levels of school funding. Personal income is the best and most consistent explainer of these interstate differences. Income is key, far outweighing social, demographic, and even racial variables in importance. High income states are able to finance public education better; and they can do it with lower school taxes.

The State Decision to Adopt a Lottery

Again, in the two analyses that addressed the lottery adoption question only one variable was determined to be significant: per capita income. Income explained 27 percent of the variance in whether or not a state operated a lottery in 1987. States with high levels of wealth, as measured by the personal income statistic, are thus more likely to be lottery states. Percent non-white, urbanization and population density, private school enrollments, whether the state's population is old or young, high school completions—none of these mattered significantly in states' lottery decisions.

It is ironic that lotteries are operated and rationalized to "help" schools in those states where personal income levels are generally higher than the national average, and where tax effort levels are sometimes lower. Yet it is often the wealthiest states, with high absolute tax burdens, which have turned to lotteries as an alternative means of public finance. As Filer et al., (1988) explain:

> Some legislators have realized that taxes have reached critically high levels and that further tax increases would erode voter support in ever increasing numbers. In such states, legislators have considered a lottery as an alternative source of state revenue in lieu of higher sales or income taxes.

There are other indicators of states' lottery inclinations that we might have chosen to study, but there were reasons for not expanding the number of predictor variables (see Appendix B). The inclusion of a variable in our study for "region of the country" almost surely would have produced statistical significance. State size seems to play a role, as perhaps do some of the more subtle social and religious factors discussed by Berry (1987) and Elazar (1972). With the passage of time, more of the low income, politically "traditional" states in Elazar's terms, have enacted lotteries. It will be interesting to see which states are early adopters of video lotteries and still newer forms of gambling now being considered.

By no means do we feel we have fully accounted for all the reasons behind lottery adoption, but of the following we do feel quite sure. Lotteries reflect, in some very rough and indirect sense, the public's perception of the tax burden (Allen, 1991).

School Support and States' Lottery Status

Simple correlation indicates that there was a positive relationship between the presence of an education lottery in 1987, state-local school spending, and the total size of the aid package. States which claim that their lotteries enhanced the funding of public schools had a higher mean level of support as measured by per pupil state-local expenditures.

This may provide some solace to lottery proponents; however, the finding is less significant than it appears at first glance. In concert with other data, a claim that lotteries influence state aid or school spending cannot be supported. Furthermore, lottery states actually used a smaller *share* of their wealth for education than non-lottery states did in 1987. Once per capita income is statistically controlled, the presence of a lottery cannot account for a significant amount of interstate variation in school support. Lottery states were able to spend more for schools than other states because they were rich states, not because they ran lotteries.

It is true that statistical controls of the type used in this study always raise methodological issues. In a narrow mathematical sense, it is impossible to say that a particular group of states spends more because it is rich or spends more because it runs lotteries. Here we assume that state wealth is a long-term prior condition. It is wealthy states which adopt lotteries in advance of other states, not lotteries which make states wealthy. There simply is no theoretical or empirical evidence to support the latter.

An additional, more directly statistical observation pertains too. Since our model explains low to moderate amounts of variance in school support and tax effort, the lottery variable has maximum opportunity to account for unexplained variance. If state lotteries had an important impact, then it would be reasonable to expect that the lottery should emerge as a significant predictor in at least one of the four regression equations. In fact, lotteries don't add significant predictive power to any of them.

Lotteries had explanatory "space"; they simply had very little or no explanatory "power." This finding is paramount. The fact that lottery revenues have little if any predictive power suggests that states are not likely to enhance public education significantly by implementing the "lottery-for-education" proposals espoused by some politicians and lottery advocates. The findings of this study, in conjunction with those discussed in Chapter 4, strongly suggest that state lottery revenues do not help schools.

The Claim that Lottery Revenues Go for School Uses

Not all states claim that lottery revenues enhance school funding. A separate set of analyses was therefore done on two groups of lottery states – those that claim funds are used partly or entirely for schools, and those that claim the money goes elsewhere. Do states that claim to use lottery revenues for public schools demonstrate higher levels of educational support or effort than states that claim the money goes for other things? To address this question t-tests were used.

In no analysis did the "lottery-for-education" claim make any difference. States that claim to use their lottery money for schools were indistinguishable from those states that have lotteries, but purport to send the money elsewhere.

This finding has considerable significance in the political debate. Lottery proponents frequently try to enlist advocates among the education community based on the promise that the schools will "win too." This study can support no such expectations.

WHAT DOES HAPPEN TO LOTTERY REVENUES?

This study appears to be the first research endeavor to consider the impact of lottery revenues on support and effort for public education, K–12, on a nationwide scale. We were interested in lotteries' effects on school finance. The issue of the ultimate disposition of lottery revenues is, strictly speaking, beyond the scope of our data analysis. Together with the substantial body of literature available, our data offers a logical vehicle for interpreting the overall significance of lottery revenues.

In absolute terms, lotteries contribute large amounts to education both directly through earmarking and indirectly through state general funds. However, based on the research presented here, it is accurate to say that lotteries do not have a significant impact when states are ranked according to per pupil amounts of state aid or per pupil state-local expenditures. Similarly, lotteries do not appear to play an important role in spending effort. When controlling for the influence of other more important determinants of interstate support, states which use lotteries to enhance educational funding do not demonstrate higher levels of spending.

There seem to be at least four possible explanations for this state of affairs.

(1) Our model is inadequate.

(2) Lottery revenues substitute for other tax receipts.

(3) Lottery revenues are financing other services but not the public schools.

(4) Lotteries (together with other forms of gambling) impose excess burdens on the economy, reducing economic growth.

With regard to number one, it is true that our research model implicitly posits an unheard claim, *not* the one lottery advocates make. Lottery advocates claim the following: "Institute or expand lotteries in state X and we'll get you more money for schools in that state." Our study posits a state *comparison* and asks: "Was school finance enhanced in lottery versus non-lottery jurisdictions?" A lottery advocate might respond, "We never claimed lotteries would put state X's spending above other states. We couched our claims entirely in terms of state X alone."

To "voice" our claim, let us be explicit. If lottery advocates make financial enhancement claims in state after state — and they have — and if they have been making such claims since the 1960s — and they have — it is reasonable to assume that lottery states will, by now, be financing schools better than non-lottery states for reasons assignable to the lottery, if advocates' claims have any validity.

Our model is sufficiently sensitive to pick up even small differences in support and effort for education, *if* differences appear systematically across states and *if* differences are independent of existing social, political, demographic, and economic variations among the states. As discussed in Chapter 3, the authors acknowledge the limits of most empirical measurements in the social sciences. Our own measures have limitations also. The model isn't capable of teleological certitude. If one or two lottery states spend more for one or two years but other states spend less and most spend the same, the model won't pick that up. If log linear regressions or some other technique not employed here would produce a different result, nothing would please us more than to see researchers try them.

As it stands, however, our findings essentially corroborate other studies of specific states which use different designs (Hartwig, 1987; Stewart, 1987; Borg and Mason, 1988, 1990; Stark et al., 1991). If lottery funds comprise such a small portion of state education revenues that they are statistically undetectable, they surely must have no practical effect either.

A second possibility is that lottery revenues may be used for the reduction of other taxes. A third possibility is that the revenues may be used to finance other services. Both of these possibilities are based on the concepts of earmarking and fungibility discussed in Chapter 1. Substitution effects are inevitable whenever earmarking devotes resources to a function that normally receives a large amount of money. Economists are nearly unanimous on this point (Tax Foundation, 1965; Gold et al., 1990; Fabricius and Snell, 1990). Substitution is the most widely held explanation as to why lottery revenues don't help the schools.

Schools are, of course, a very popular public service, well established in American public finance. Though educational finance controversies develop from time to time in every state, they usually involve increasing conventional taxes. There is a conviction that—in the abstract—schools need more money. Lottery advocates use schools as a rationalization. A lottery earmarked for abortions, drug addicts, or more middle class entitlement programs might not sell quite as many tickets! And so these purposes are seldom linked to the lottery. To the extent that tax substitution does not occur, lottery revenues probably finance the less popular, and in this sense more marginal, public services.

A fourth and final possibility is that lotteries, along with other forms of gambling, impose burdens that reduce economic growth. Both private sector and public sector revenues decline as the public becomes consumed in passing money around, not creating new wealth.

This alternative is conceptually quite different from an implied or expressed political decision to use lottery funds for reducing taxes or financing public services. The entire economy is affected. Very possibly we end up with higher conventional taxes *and* a lottery. The argument has some theoretical support and considerable intuitive appeal, but at this stage there is little evidence for it (Clotfelter and Cook, 1989).

THE LOTTERY'S ROLE IN THE CONTEMPORARY SOCIAL STRUCTURE

If lottery proponents make unfounded claims, one may wonder why we have the games at all. The response is, of course, that for many people they are an intrinsically enjoyable activity, a simple pleasure, an enjoyable pastime. It is, of course, not the money that people want. It's the things money buys.

> The next best thing to a fortune is the chance at a fortune. . . . To purchase a lottery ticket in a lottery, indeed, is to buy a kind of fiction in which oneself is a hero. It is to see oneself, in one's mind's eye, happy and rich, free from all the cares and anxieties involved in earnng a living, able to buy a cottage in the country, to take as long a holiday as one wishes, and so forth. It may not be the most heroic of ideals, but it is among the most innocent. (Devereux, 1980)

Even small winnings have the appeal of being surplus to one's personal budget. The money can be "blown" without remorse, or it can be used to fulfill long-standing material wants and needs. A problem is that gambling for purely economic motives can also have a desperate character, if it is abused.

Lotteries can be viewed as a legitimate protest against rationality. Rational behavior has great prominence in our society. It is what Devereux (1980) terms, "a structural imperative of capitalism," though one suspects it is just as imperative in socialism or other economic systems. Gambling is perhaps the only form of socially sanctioned activity in which luck plays the dominant and defining role.

Playing the lottery seriously is distinctly irrational from the scientific point of view, but not from everyone's point of view. Chapters 2 and 3 reviewed the production of "dream books" containing lucky numbers and their modern day equivalents based on statistical probabilities. A certain segment of the population feels that choosing winning numbers is not blind luck, that skill is involved.

But even if winning is considered pure luck, lotteries put everyone on a perfectly equal footing. Men and women, blacks and whites, rich and poor, Ph.D.'s and grade school dropouts — if you can keep track of your ticket you have an equal chance to win. Never mind that, rationally, the chances of winning are very very slight, and that different groups have different propensities to play.

For many people gambling offers the thrill of play. Lotteries are less engaging than the active forms of gambling such as roulette, craps, or blackjack. It is generally thought that the active games are more likely than lotteries to lead to impulsive and excessive betting. Lotteries have made the bettor wait—at least until that evening's draw. Such reasoning provides the justification for legalizing lotteries in jurisdictions where most other forms of gambling are still prohibited.

Although traditional lotteries engage players less intensely than some other gambling games, this may not be true in the future. With the passage of time, there is less and less distinction between lotteries and the more active games. Video lottery terminals, with their bells and lights, are designed expressly to encourage play by engaging the bettor. Like casinos, the VLT machine provides instant knowledge of results. And also like casinos, these instant results allow gamblers an instant chance to play again—something that can snowball into compulsive excessive betting, or even full-blown addiction.

Does society have the right, or the duty, to save people from themselves? The widely respected economist Dick Netzer (Anon., "On a Roll . . .," 1990) argues, "Criticism of legal gambling smacks of nanny ordering the retired and working folks. . . . We the affluent don't want you the unwashed to enjoy your simple pleasures." Arguably, since children are prohibited from buying lottery tickets and engaging in other gambling acts, society has fulfilled its paternalist role. Adults should be left alone.

We take seriously the libertarian argument raised by writers such as Netzer. But here again lotteries are a special case. They are the only form of gambling actively promoted by the state. In relation to the size of the total bet, lotteries' contributions to state coffers far exceed those of any other game. The state's multiple role as owner, promoter, major beneficiary, and regulator is, to say the least, unique.

COMPARING PUBLIC AND PRIVATE BEHAVIOR

The gambling impulse is as old as human society. It has been the subject of analysis by professional social scientists and trenchant observers of the human condition.

Gambling is a not a highly regarded activity. At best it is seen as a relatively harmless pastime. At its most negative, gambling promotes serious pathologies in a percentage of the population. The heaviest gamblers are usually society's most marginal people: the poor, the lonely, the destitute, and those who have suffered social or economic reverses. These facts about gambling are well accepted and widely known. There is a legitimate and long-standing dispute about society's role in its regulation.

Nearly all analyses deal with the demand side of the equation – the characteristics of the individual gambler. Discussions, debates, and investigations of gambling are organized in terms that may be deemed individualist. The appropriate social role – that is, the government's role – is contested based upon gambling's effects on individuals.

Yet in today's world, it is the state that determines gambling's "supply side." This is especially true of the lottery, the one form of gaming most fully under state control. To us, the more interesting question is not, "Why do people gamble?" but rather, "Why does the state now encourage them to do so?"

At the outset it should be reemphasized that government involvement in gambling did not begin *de novo* when the state of New Hampshire authorized a lottery in 1964. Chapter 1 discussed lotteries around the world; some of these predate World War II. Chapter 2 reviewed the history of the games in modern Europe, and colonial and nineteenth century America. Though lotteries were phased out in America in the later years of the last century, bingo, horse racing, and Nevada's casino gambling have existed through most of the present one.

What is new about the present era, we argue, is the intimate nature of the lottery's connection with the modern state. None of the characteristics of modern day lotteries is unprecedented. All have their roots in earlier versions of the games. The most distinctive characteristics of contemporary lotteries are these.

- Lotteries are accepted as an arm of government.
- Lotteries operate continuously, month after month, and year after year.
- Lottery funds are routinely incorporated into state budgets.
- Winning is largely dissociated from the worthiness of the cause.
- The revenue is used by those who authorize the lottery.

- Beneficiaries of the lottery also write the rules under which they may be conducted and promoted.
- All is justified as a painless way to raise necessary public revenue.

We will examine each of these individually.

Lotteries Are Accepted as an Arm of Government

Earlier lotteries for private purposes contrast with today's lotteries for the government. Today we do not have the Virginia Company's lotteries or the Literature Lottery, we have a California lottery or an Ontario lottery. Whatever its administrative structure, the modern lottery is viewed as an enterprise that is part of the state.

This ties the fortunes of the lottery to the state in an unprecedented way. Instead of a game, lotteries become a tax, and very likely a regressive one: poor people spend disproportionate shares of their income on it. Government says it uses the money to finance good causes, but no evidence exists to affirm the claim.

When normal ethical standards—say those that government applies to private industry—are applied to lotteries, the comparisons are invidious. People who hold negative opinions of lotteries may come to hold negative opinions of the governments that sponsor them.

Lotteries Operate Continuously, Month after Month, and Year after Year

In the past, lotteries weren't routine. They were given licenses to operate for a time—what we would call today a "sunset provision." This required legislative reconsideration on a specified timetable.

Government decisions about the conduct of lotteries could be made on dual grounds—the worthiness of the cause and the morality of the operation. Administrative chicanery, changing public perceptions, and political alliances shifted lottery revenues, or eliminated them altogether. Under these conditions lotteries could never become more than a marginal revenue instrument.

In the modern state, lotteries have no sunset provisions. Government cannot separate the conduct of the lottery from its own interest in it.

Lottery Funds Are Routinely Incorporated into State Budgets

This follows directly from the previous two points. Rather than financing exceptional or temporary activities, rather than dedicating funds to specific purposes outside government budgets, today's lottery revenues are estimated in advance by government finance specialists and are built into the state budget.

This feature appears to give them a permanent place in America's tax structure. No state with a lottery has ever considered abolishing it; such a move would mean higher taxes. We're hooked; the discussion now taking place deals with expansion of lotteries and addition of more forms of gambling.

Winning Is Largely Dissociated from the Worthiness of the Cause

It is at least a tenable proposition that charity raffles build interest in the good works of the sponsor. You know what the cause is. The cause may be pursued only if the lottery is successful. You buy a ticket if you believe in the cause, and winning is a sort of bonus.

Of course, in the modern state lottery, this is the rationale for invoking the public schools or other good causes: "Our Schools Win Too." In fact, however, lotteries could never hope to make up more than a tiny share of state education costs. Ticket buyers can never really know where the money goes. Government becomes the sole judge of worthy causes.

The Revenue Is Used by Those Who Authorize the Lottery

State operation of the lottery is sometimes justified as a way to preempt others from conducting them. This rationale assumes the state is above mean or selfish acts. *Only* the state should be allowed to conduct and profit from a lottery, something which has a long history of abuse in the wrong hands.

The problem is that state agencies and state policy makers are not generally superheroes. They occasionally suffer from bouts of selfishness, venality, or just plain blindness like the rest of us. Revenues go into the state's general fund for whatever uses are specified by the legislature. And meeting public needs is what gets legislators reelected. The rationale for the modern state lottery always requires legislators to distinguish the public interest from their private ones, something very hard to do.

Beneficiaries of the Lottery Also Write the Rules under Which They May Be Conducted and Promoted

Not only do legislatures use lottery revenues at their own discretion, they also write the rules for conducting games.

As it stands, however, modern state lotteries are run like a private monopoly enterprise. Just like any private business, the main objective is to maximize revenue. Advertising and promotion are designed to stimulate demand for tickets, and a high takeout rate assures large state profits.

Lotteries might be run to provide an enjoyable consumer service. If so, the state's takeout would not be so large. Or, lotteries might be designed to satisfy what is called "unstimulated demand" for gaming. If so, there would be little or no advertising, minimal newspaper and television coverage (Clotfelter and Cook, 1990). But the modern state lottery has, as its prime purpose, the production of revenue. Television, billboards, and the print media are available, and so they are heavily used for promotion.

All Is Justified as a Painless Way to Raise Necessary Public Revenue

All lotteries are conducted to raise revenues, but government operation makes a difference. Giving to charity events is entirely voluntary. The state, on the other hand, is sovereign. It is the only agent in society which is empowered to exact revenues from its members. Normally this is done through the tax system. When government resorts to raising revenue through gambling profits, the state acts like something it is not—a free and voluntary "pay if you want" kind of enterprise.

Suppose that we knew of individuals who gambled routinely, who were always on the make for a game, urging others to gamble also. They fixed the games so they couldn't lose. And they justified their behavior on the grounds that they couldn't stop now, since they were doing their family a favor—gambling winnings were absolutely necessary to balance the family budget.

If we knew of such *individuals* we would say that they had a serious problem. We would easily distinguish these individuals from the occasional recreational gambler. We would view the gambling act itself as indicative of deep-seated problems in personality structure. If we had a psychological bent, we would try to understand the whole pathology. We would not expect that injunctions to "stop it" would get very far. But the kinds of pathologies we recognize in persons, we have failed to recognize in the body politic.

STATE LOTTERIES AS A PUBLIC PATHOLOGY

Chapter 1 illustrated how the revenue imperative of states has grown apace. In composite, governments' share of the economy has risen by about one-third over the lifetime of middle-aged Americans (Advisory Commission on Intergovernmental Relations, 1991). Most people today think the size of government should be reduced. Since people consider (different) government activities to be illegitimate, they are unwilling to pay conventional sales, income, and property taxes in the full amount required. But one person's white elephants are someone else's sacred cows, and no one wants his or her particular program cut.

Lotteries entered the picture as a "voluntary tax," ostensibly bridging the gap between what citizens want from their government and what they are willing to pay. This is their political appeal. Lotteries may not be a particularly ethical revenue source, but at least lotteries *are* a revenue source. They shield us, a little, from government's relentless demands for more sales, income, and property taxes. They do not cost money; they raise it. Or at least so most people believe.

In the sponsorship of gambling, government creates a new dilemma for itself. By employing lotteries as a revenue instrument, government engages in an activity which many view as wrong. Government thereby undermines its own role. If this analysis has any validity, then a government's resort to sponsorship of gambling is a sign of popular disenchantment with government itself.

The first point to make in this regard is that government is *sovereign*. It is the institution in society which makes the rules by which individuals and other institutions — schools, churches, business, etc. — must live. In order to be successful at this task, democratic government must have popular support. There must be a very widespread perception that the rules made by the sovereign are *legitimate*. That is, the rules must be regarded as legal, not merely in the formal sense that they are enacted by a legislature. People must view the rules as right, just, and proper. If rules are unjust or improper, the government's own ethical standing is impaired.

In its quest for revenues, the government has fashioned lottery rules that chiefly benefit itself. Government itself sets the rules for production, advertising, and sales. It keeps the bulk of the proceeds. In short, it acts as both entrepreneur and rule maker—both profiteer and sovereign.

"Sold" to the electorate on the basis that they will reduce other taxes or provide better services, lotteries do neither. They become another one of government's false promises. This analysis, however, is not intended to suggest that lotteries have no lasting effects. In fact, there are two. First of all, that portion of the citizenry which views lotteries as morally wrong is further disaffected from government, becoming even less likely to support new taxes of any type. Secondly, the claim that lotteries add new revenue further raises the hopes of those who want still more and newer spending programs. Lotteries raise people's expectations of their government while making it still less likely that citizens will pay the taxes necessary to support those expectations.

What is the net effect? In the short run the effect is likely to be institution of still more and newer forms of gambling—an eventuality we see taking shape today. In the longer run, state lotteries undermine the government's role as an ethical sovereign. Government simply makes the rules for its own advantage.

CURRENT REFORM PROPOSALS

There is no lack of proposals to change state lotteries. Abolition of the games is a theoretical possibility, but for reasons already discussed, abolition seems unlikely. Additional gambling legalizations seem much more probable. Proposals directed toward that end are seriously discussed in state legislatures. We no longer debate whether to hold lotteries at all; we debate, rather, what kind of lotteries to hold (Clotfelter and Cook, 1989). For these reasons the remaining discussion deals with reform, not abolition.

Privatization is one reform discussed briefly in Chapter 3. States might authorize several private companies to operate lotteries, not just to supply tickets, advertising, and terminals as they do now. Many games could operate simultaneously, under different sponsors. Or governments could expand their lottery offerings. A national lottery could be implemented along Canadian lines to compete with the lotteries in each state (province). Theoretically, state statutes could authorize each locality or school district to hold its own lottery. States could grant multiple licenses to a variety of companies offering competing games.

Privatization would fulfill its promise of more consumer choice, and would theoretically make operations more efficient. Competition and efficiency would stimulate more demand. But more lottery play is not something we see as benign. If lotteries came under private or local public control, we suspect state policy makers would agree with our view. Stricter state controls on licensure and advertising would inevitably reduce choice and efficiency below what a perfectly free market would allow. Controls would also undermine consumer appeal and efficiency—the very reasons for a choice in the first place.

Privatization also raises the specter of chicanery and criminality. Lottery history, most of which involved private operators, is not promising in this regard. Computers have been successful in reducing lottery criminality to a minimum in the state-operated games, so there is reason to suppose they could do the same for privately operated ones.

In its favor, the privatization alternative recognizes that state lotteries, viewed as an excise tax, impose higher burdens than do taxes on liquor, cigarettes, or any other "sin" items. Like other sumptuary taxes, government's exactions from the lottery probably fall more heavily on the poor. There is no ethical reason why lottery players should pay more than smokers and drinkers. The reasons for it are entirely historical. Taxes on alcohol, casinos, etc., predate the modern welfare state. Lotteries had the misfortune to be legalized only after the state's revenue demands had already become enormous. Illegal numbers racketeers were thought to keep about half the wagers made. Government's 50 percent share was considered the maximum possible: that rate would permit the legalized games to compete with the illegal ones on a par. Lottery players, the main victims of the present policy, aren't yet well organized. Asserting players' "rights" to a greater share of the bet seems dubious.

The virtues of privatization are, from the state's point of view, precisely its defects. As with any monopolist, competition will reduce the state's revenues over time. Private companies (or possibly state and local lotteries) will function as profit seekers at the expense of the competition. They will promise to raise the payout rate, thereby creating massive public support among players. All operators eventually will have to go along because the leading ones will advertise. A privatized lottery might do for players what they themselves have not done: reduce the tax price of this particular "sin." The companies would get a bigger share; the players would get a bigger share; and the state's current operation would lose revenue.

As it stands, sale of tickets across state lines remains illegal. States have successfully preserved their monopolies. We view privatization as a most unlikely possibility, unless payout rates become a political issue.

The most widely discussed alternative deals with reforming the games, while keeping them state owned and operated. There are three possibilities.

(1) States could voluntarily choose to return more of the players' revenue, making the lottery tax no heavier than other sin taxes.

(2) States could elect to cut down their advertising and promotion. They could distribute smaller prizes to more players, thereby eliminating the frenetic buying that accompanies newspaper articles describing huge lotto jackpots.

(3) States could tinker with the nature of their public controls, making lottery agencies more autonomous public corporations (Borg and Mason, 1990; Clotfelter and Cook, 1990; Vance, 1986; Commission on the Review of National Policy toward Gambling, 1976).

Underlying this set of proposals is an ambiguous fiscal situation. Is the lottery to be viewed as a tax? If so, it is regressive. Or is the lottery more appropriately viewed as an inexpensive leisure time activity? Viewed as leisure, lotteries may be acceptable. We wouldn't close amusement parks or movie theaters because poor people spend a larger share of their money at them than rich people do.

Even if the lottery is a tax, tickets are a discretionary purchase. Is the state morally obligated to structure the games so that lottery players do as well as dice or blackjack players? Clotfelter and Cook (1989) argue that states should do this, but as discussed above, "equity" among forms of gambling is presently not a major concern.

Is the lottery inherently immoral, or is it morally neutral? If it is immoral, then the government should not encourage play through advertising and the prize structure. The alternative, moral neutrality, suggests that anything government can do to promote a ticket sale may be permissible. Underlying the whole discussion are deep convictions which touch on religious beliefs.

Beliefs of particular faiths, or any faith at all, have rarely provided a basis for policy implementation in America. We are a pragmatic people. Our history suggests that an anti-gambling consensus traditionally develops from the discovery of widespread criminality. Disaffection with the entire gambling enterprise slowly sets in as evidence of dishonesty mounts.

Things seem to be different this time. There is no widespread criminality associated with lotteries or any other form of gambling today, and there is no reason to suspect it will emerge. Big governments, corporations, and even small retail establishments are making too much money within the laws they have helped to write. They have absolutely no incentive to operate outside them. If criminality were wide spread, the gambling establishment—government and business—would lead the fight against it. Considerations of a pragmatic morality, one based on the evil consequences of gambling, provide an unlikely basis for change.

Lottery advertising and promotion are often assailed, but we live in a society where nearly all other commodities are advertised and promoted. There is very little hard evidence of harmful consequences from lotteries. Doubtless some proportion of the population has a serious gambling problem, but the involvement of lotteries in the problem is unknown and undocumented. Casino gaming is thought to be the more major culprit, if there is a culprit at all. Even if we did know that a certain proportion of the population had serious gambling problems, and that those problems derived from lotteries, this would still have to be weighed against the matter of stopping other people's harmless fun.

Proposals calling for public corporations in lottery operation presumably shield government from any sordid gambling associations while encouraging more rigorous government oversight in advertising and promotion. Descriptive studies of public corporation lotteries haven't detected many distinguishing features (Anon., "Kentucky Creates Unique . . .," 1989; Vance, 1986). Discussions along these lines are more likely to be a smoke screen than a real reform.

If our notion of an emerging pathology in public spending has validity, these reforms are most unlikely. All of them would require states to deny themselves lottery revenues. Returning more money to lottery players would obviously reduce state revenues in the short run, putting added pressure on sales, income, and property taxes. These broad-based and compulsory taxes were precisely the ones that lotteries were thought to relieve in the first place. Reducing advertising and promotion and tampering with the prize structure would likewise hurt ticket sales. Play would be less enticing.

Conventional proposals to reform the lottery resemble warnings to an addicted gambler to "stop it." They are likely to have about as much effect.

Our intent here is to couch the operations of the modern state lottery in a broader context of principle and ideology. Lotteries achieve significance not through the details of their operation but through their implications for the conduct of statecraft. Though opinions differ on the morality of lotteries, almost no one believes they should be an integral part of government, depended upon to finance vital services such as schools.

We return to the central dilemma of modern governments: they provide so many services wanted by so few. Everyone has to pay, and people are increasingly unwilling to do so (Bosanquet, 1983). There is so much "good" to be done and so little money to do it. We simply accept the fact that states will act badly in order to do good. A collective blind spot takes shape. This is the spot which lotteries now occupy.

OUR PROPOSALS FOR LOTTERY REFORM

Modern government is the organizer, administrator, regulator, and chief financial beneficiary of the lottery. We view these multiple roles as an ethical problem with practical consequences, part of a larger problem in the modern welfare state. We acknowledge that presently, few people have made this connection, but as lotteries drift toward more extreme forms we hope their true nature will soon become apparent.

Two Proposals for Reform of the Lottery

Our proposals are simple. First, all objective measures of school finances indicate that lotteries do not help. To support this claim we rely not only on this study. Studies using different methodologies, states, and time periods, report the same findings. The weight of theoretical and empirical evidence from the field of economics supports the findings.

Controverting the evidence, many state governments claim the opposite—lotteries operate for the benefit of schools. They have made false claims for decades, and they continue to do so. For too many years the public schools have been an unwitting accomplice in states' lottery advertising campaigns. Schools must be eliminated from the advertising and political debate about lotteries. Accordingly, we propose that in every state where school financial claims have been made, the following statement, or a reasonable approximation thereof, be put on each lottery ticket and terminal. *The state of 'X' has determined that lotteries may not provide improved levels of school funding.* This would simply be truth in advertising. The word "may" suggests a "weight of the evidence" approach. It allows for the possibility that somewhere sometime an isolated study may reach a different conclusion.

Such a step deliberately emulates the warning labels on packs of cigarettes. For years we were told that cigarettes "taste good." Research established that smoking cigarettes is associated with an increased risk of contracting fatal diseases. Government decided that smokers ought to know the truth. In the case of cigarettes, the government acted sensibly. Now the question is whether government can act sensibly when its own revenue base is at stake.

We do not suppose that such a warning will halt lottery sales or that it necessarily should. Like Dick Netzer we worry a little about government becoming a "nanny." But we confess we worry more about government becoming a snake oil salesman. It is a tenable proposition that adults should have the right to gamble. It is not a tenable proposition that government should encourage them to do it by making false claims about gambling's role in aiding education.

We note that even within lotteries themselves there is a precedent to truth in advertising. Some states now require that the odds of winning be displayed on tickets and on advertising. We hope that a similar notification about schools will create a different climate of understanding among ticket buyers, and among members of the public at large. Long-standing false claims from authoritative sources like the state cannot be redressed easily. But educators must try. Among all professions, education is the one that lays the best claim to the disinterested pursuit of truth.

We have no doubt that, if a warning statement were ever seriously considered, states or the industry would commission studies to "prove" that lotteries help schools. We say, "Let those games begin." The weight of the evidence will always be on our side.

As shown in Chapter 5, lottery revenues are substantial. If all states that operated lotteries in 1987 had used the money for elementary-secondary education, lottery contributions in nine of these states would have exceeded per pupil federal school aid. This consideration prompted us to analyze alternative fiscal arrangements assuring that lottery money would flow to schools, as advertised.

For earmarking to work, the following two conditions must be met.

- There must be separate fund accounting with the money dedicated to a specified beneficiary.
- The service benefitted must be financed entirely, or almost entirely, with the revenues from the dedicated source.

As soon as other revenue sources are made available, the problem of fungibility reemerges.

It is true that lottery revenues have grown rapidly over time. But in specific states in specific years they do not grow. We can think of no aspect of public education that should be submitted to the vagaries of lottery funding. If a particular curriculum, building project, or other educational activity is important enough to be financed publicly, it is important enough to be financed properly—through the regular tax system. For both technical and ethical reasons, trying to make earmarks work is not a viable possibility, however well intentioned legislators may be. This further reinforces the need for a government warning on lottery tickets.

A drawback to this proposal is that it might indirectly encourage governments to make similar political claims for public services other than education. States might claim that the money goes for health, eldercare, or other good causes. Education should not foist its problem onto other public sector activities. Again, if such activities are important enough to be financed publicly, they too should be financed through the regular tax system. This brings us to our second, and absolute preferred, policy alternative: *the states should renounce any financial interest whatsoever in lotteries.*

Only through doing this, we feel, can the state reclaim its social legitimacy. Gambling generally, and lotteries specifically, are rejected as morally dubious by a substantial segment of the population. The state has offered, as its sole moral justification for running lotteries, the argument that if they don't do it someone else will. A dubious activity would be left in private hands; and so the sovereign must act preemptively.

But an ethical sovereign is above the fray, always acting in the public interest. If these facts—and only these—were relevant, we could stop with the first recommendation on warning labels. But we cannot. In conducting lotteries, states are risking their own legitimacy.

If so, then a clearer view for the state emerges. The state must regulate gambling but not benefit from it. When the state organizes lotteries, benefits financially, and writes the rules for conducting them, the state undermines itself. As the sovereign, the state is the only institution in society able to set the rules. Many other, better means of raising revenues are at its disposal.

Renunciation of lottery profits sets the appropriate framework for states' lottery management. It could abolish them (though we consider that alternative is unlikely). States could turn lotteries over to private operators with careful regulation. Or the state could continue to organize and conduct lotteries as they do now, but without benefitting from any profits.

Whichever mode of organization the state selects, this much is key. Separation of the beneficiaries from the rule makers is the only way to deal legitimately with the complex ethical and technical issues gambling presents. Even then, we do not assume there can ever be a total and complete wall. Individual gamblers and the industry will always be able to put in their oar. But under present circumstances, states must be viewed as a special interest too. The sovereign must reclaim its unique place as arbiter of the debate, not the beneficiary of one side in it. Without this change, any lottery policy the government imposes will inevitably be viewed as half way, equivocal, and very possibly rigged.

Operationally, the state has two means of effecting the result. First, it could return all lottery profits to the players. Second, it could turn any profits over to private charities. Both of these alternatives raise major moral issues and procedural problems in themselves. Here we touch only on the main ones.

As for procedure, the designation of "profits" would require careful attention from accountants. If the state's renunciation of profits became little more than moving lottery revenues from the bottom line into the category of "operating cost," little would be accomplished.

On the moral side, return of the gambler's full share raises new issues. Would that encourage more gambling? Is it better for society if all gamblers know that, in the aggregate, they will lose? We suspect that among all gamblers, lottery (and bingo) players like the idea of "doing good, by trying to do well." In the minds of many players the "contribution" aspect gives their play a morally redemptive character. From the viewpoint of both the individual and the society it is perhaps unwise to eliminate this aspect of the game.

This brings us to the idea of giving lottery profits to private charities. These charities assist the state when they do good works. And yet the work of private charities, by definition, is not quite as vital as the work of the state. They are without the government's powers to compel revenues through a tax system, making them different entities. Charitable giving satisfies any generous dispositions that gamblers may have. The interests of the sovereign are satisfied by not returning players' entire wager, and gambling would be kept within the bounds of moderation.

This alternative brings us to our discussion of the last feature of the modern state lottery, the one feature which we consider to be good. Lotteries are very small revenue producers in relation to all the state does. No government agency or private charity is pressing for a special share. Today's lotteries benefit no one in particular except the state legislators who appropriate the profits annually in the budget process.

Giving charity a share in the proceeds offers potential problems reminiscent of Eliphalet Nott (see Chapter 2). His biography serves in this book as a cautionary tale for modern government. Nott was so convinced of the moral worth of his causes that he built a system of lotteries to finance them, but there was never enough money to do all the good things that needed to be done. If lottery revenues provide a significant share of income to any charity, charities could be counted on to lobby for more lotteries, all in the name of their noble cause.

We do not want to return to those bad old days. We think noncorrupting charitable distributions are possible. Monies could go in different amounts to a very wide variety of private charities. If the amounts were small and very irregular, one hopes no charity would become dependent on them. Of course, government should not determine the appropriation levels for specific organizations.

The United Fund provides one possible model. Lotteries of certain foreign governments operate in this way. The public's moderate gambling demands are met within the moral standards expected of government. In any arrangements detailing this matter, the guiding principle must be that lottery revenues represent a sort of tainted money. Profits must be disposed of in ways that influence private actions and public policies minimally.

LOTTERIES AND SCHOOL FINANCE REFORM

By the mid-1990s the annual percentage growth in public school spending slowed markedly, continuing the trends discussed in the first chapter. The reduced rate of spending growth was due partly to a declining rate of inflation in the U.S. Slowing inflation did not necessarily mean that schools were worse off in an absolute sense. Their revenues were growing more slowly, but so were their costs. Everyone's expectations for income growth were ratcheted down. The inflation improvements may fairly be said to be a long run benefit to the nation and to its educational systems.

Other economic changes were not so benign. The "rolling recessions" which had hit large sections of the Midwest and Southwest in the 1980s had, by the 1990s, moved on to hit the two coasts. California and the Northeast were particularly hurt by reductions in expenditures for national defense. In these regions, the recessions impacted the ability of state governments to provide school funding increases. Nor could the national government make up the slack. Cuts in defense spending may someday lead to increased federal spending on schools and other social services, but the continuing large federal budget deficits indicate that day is well in the future.

A third factor limiting school spending increases is the rise in "entitlement spending" at all levels of government. Entitlements are laws which mandate automatic spending increases in designated government programs, usually according to the rate of inflation. (In the case of health care, entitlement spending has grown at a rate much higher than inflation.) Government tax receipts, on the other hand, ordinarily grow in line with the overall economy. If, for example, inflation is 3 percent while economic growth is 2 percent, governments must either raise taxes, fund entitlements through reduced allocations to non-entitlement programs, or both.

Though state school aid formulas frequently contain entitlement-like provisions, these provisions are often abrogated. Effective entitlements are aimed at retirees, the elderly, the sick, or the disabled – they are not aimed at the majority of the school age population. Apparently the public feels that living standards of the aged and infirm should be relatively insulated from the vagaries of the economy. Youth inevitably will be living in the future; schools must be subject to economic realities. Or at least this is one interpretation for the conspicuous failure of education to fall under government's entitlement umbrella.

Finally, it may be the case that fundamental disagreements over the direction of school policy have hurt the aggregate level of school funding. The numerous educational reforms proposed and debated in recent years are often seen as ineffectual, only theoretical, or even counterproductive. Regardless of their efficacy, recent educational reforms – except the lottery – have not been aimed at school revenue enhancement.

School restructuring is a case in point. Discussed briefly in Chapter 1, restructuring is a concept borrowed from the corporate world of the 1980s. For corporations, restructuring meant dropping entire lines of business, or taking on new businesses through mergers, acquisitions, and start-ups.

Restructuring relates to finance in that it is supposed to provide greater value per dollar spent. But the concept has not proven relevant to education. A school cannot simply decide to drop the teaching of mathematics or history because it doesn't teach these subjects well. Likewise schools cannot simply decide, as private businesses can, to make shoes or doughnuts because these would produce a profit. The services required of schools, and the conditions under which they must provide those services, militate against restructuring along business lines, and so applications of the concept usually revolve around theoretical considerations of "effective organization" (Murphy, 1990).

For public schools, restructuring possibilities seem highly limited. Discussions have been largely internal to the school establishment and have not led to many new forms of public support for schools, moral or financial.

Another proposed reform relates to the implementation of national standards for education. National standards would entail a uniform school curriculum across the fifty states and a single set of qualifications for America's teachers, although these might be voluntary at first

(The National Center for Effective Schools, 1993). Detailed proposals for national standards have not yet been fully developed in the United States; however, many foreign countries have a national curriculum, and a national teacher service along those lines being discussed here.

National standards proposals are offered with much the same goals in mind as the restructuring movement's goals – to improve the level of pupils' academic achievement, and to equalize the provision of education across poor and wealthy areas. Considered on its merits, it is not entirely clear that nationalization promotes better school achievement or greater social equity. Most foreign governments which have national standards show inconclusive results.

Regardless of educational equity and efficiency merits, improved funding is not the ostensible rationale offered by national standards advocates. In an indirect sense, the national standards movement does have the potential to provide a large one-time boost in the level of federal school aid. The idea encounters such stiff criticism from established state and local interests that states and localities probably would accept externally imposed national standards only if they received a large financial incentive to do so. Unless and until the federal government finances them, national standards are likely to remain in the discussion stage.

A third reform proposal involves allowing parents to select the school of their choice (Lieberman, 1990). This contrasts sharply with the present system, which assigns children to schools based on where they live. There is an infinite variety of school choice plans. Choice might be limited to public schools; or it might extend to private schools, religious schools, and proprietary, profit-seeking schools where the government paid all or a portion of the tuition.

Like restructuring and national standards, the school choice movement has as its broad aim the promotion of equity and efficiency in education. But choice advocates do not assume that government, acting by itself, can accomplish these aims. Instead choice advocates trust to the forces of individuals and schools operating in a free market setting. In trusting market forces rather than government, choice seems a more radical reform than the first two.

The aim of all choice plans is to redirect funding from unpopular schools to popular ones. In this sense, choice would help the finances of some individual schools, but at a cost to other schools. Consumers, and the public, would theoretically receive more value for their money.

School choice offers a far greater possibility for fundamental change. But like the first two reforms discussed here, choice does not expressly envision greater aggregate levels of school expenditure. And, in fact, in its direct "value for money" aims, school choice is remarkably like restructuring and national standards. None of the major movements of the past decade sees lack of funding as a major impediment to school improvement. These reforms do not envision that more money will, by itself, improve education.

From the viewpoint of the profession, however, spending is not irrelevant. Money buys better facilities, smaller classes, and probably, over time, a wider and better selection of candidates for teaching positions. Furthermore, educators have a direct and personal interest in more funding.

For all these reasons, public schools have, in recent years, looked increasingly to non-traditional—that is, non-tax—sources of funds. The lottery, considered as a voluntary tax, is simply one of several alternative financing methods to fund education without relying on traditional income, sales, and property taxes. Innovative methods, in addition to the lottery, are user fees, foundation grants, and enterprise activities. Each of these methods has appeal to local school administrators, teachers, and political leaders. They will be considered in turn, and then related to the lottery.

User Fees

State statutes prohibit schools from charging tuition for basic instruction; however, some schools have implemented student charges for various activities and services which they provide. Though not a new or widespread method of school finance, user fees are common enough to deserve mention.

A few states permit schools to charge for textbooks and busing. Charges for summer school and extracurricular activities are more common. Charges for food sold during the school day are considered normal. Schools with user fees often provide waivers for children from poor families.

Underlying the debate over user fees is the historic concept of American public schooling as free and available to all without charge. Should schools be able to charge some students for some services, if their parents can afford to pay? Should schools be able to deny other children certain activities based on the fact that their parents cannot or will not pay? If so, what are the limits? These questions have found no clear answer in the political arena. With the exception of charges for school lunch, user fees are very controversial.

The imposition of fees is controlled by the laws of the various states. Litigation over the practice is fairly common (Dayton and McCarthy, 1992). Cases are often decided based on what is integral to the core school program (no fees) and what is peripheral (fees permitted under certain circumstances).

Most public school activities are central. According to conventional reasoning, schools cannot produce two classes of citizens. If some children have much greater access to activities and services than other children within the same building, resentments and divisions might well develop. In general, then, equity considerations forbid the imposition of user fees.

Somewhat different considerations might obtain under certain school choice plans; costs might be uniform within schools but different among schools. School tuition may reasonably be viewed as a form of user fee. But this would indicate a radical departure from the recent past, and the possibility is not much discussed by school choice proponents. The thrust of most state legislation in school finance and other areas has gone entirely the other way in the past thirty years—toward uniformity in cost and service provision.

In the present political climate, proponents of user fees must argue that the services they provide are extras, in no way vital to the school program. This argument, by its nature, severely limits application of user fees. In the aggregate user fees have not made up any significant proportion of public school expenses in the past, and are not likely to do so in the near future.

Foundations

Private foundations sometimes give funds to public schools. In the past decade, some public schools and school systems sponsored their own foundations expressly for the purpose of soliciting funds from private sources. There are three rationales motivating foundation giving.

In a typical model, private corporations donate funds, the time of their professional staff, or products they make to schools located near plants or corporate business offices. Businesses are frequently the employers of local school graduates (or the payer of welfare bills if school leavers cannot get jobs). Many enterprises are genuinely motivated by social concerns, and for this reason inner-city schools are probably the most frequent recipients of foundation funding. For example, insurance companies in Hartford, Connecticut, fund a Saturday morning tutoring and enrichment program for that city's youth. Other programs exist in Pittsburgh, New York, and major cities throughout the nation.

In smaller cities or suburban areas, the public schools may establish their own foundations to solicit tax-deductible corporate contributions. Frequently, these entities are established to fund some specific school need, such as carpeting or a computer lab. A third rationale for foundations is the funding of enrichment programs in very well-to-do school districts. States sometimes put limits on local property taxes as they mandate equal spending across all districts. Foundation donations may allow a district to raise its spending a few dollars above a mandated ceiling.

Most school districts are not in a position to solicit private foundation funding – local businesses and individuals in most areas simply don't have the funds. In those areas where it is a possibility, foundation funding tends to be sporadic, dependent to some extent on business profits. Outlays tend to be for specific purposes, sometimes related to the donor's business. Cultivating donors tends to be labor intensive, requiring the time of school personnel to build relationships and fashion programs. Foundation aid can be important, but in general, foundations have limited application to public school education.

Enterprise Activities

The term *enterprise activity* relates to money-making businesses operated by public schools. Revenues from these activities are used to enhance the educational program.

School stores, fairs, etc., represent one typical class of activities. Students, parents, and the general public may be asked to donate goods, services, or their time. Or they may be solicited for sales of purchased or donated goods. A second type of enterprise activity is the rental of school auditoriums, stadiums, classrooms, or other facilities to out-of-school groups. A third type of enterprise activity involves the sale of tickets for school sponsored events – plays, concerts, and, especially, interscholastic athletics. All of these can contribute directly to some aspect of a school's operation.

Revenues raised from enterprise activities usually are dedicated to specific uses, e.g., the school yearbook, the pep club. These revenues may not appear in the regular school budget, and thus are not used for regular instruction. Schools are not suited to undertake substantial entrepreneurial activities and are generally prohibited by statute from developing new lines of business. Enterprise activities represent an insignificant portion of school budgets now, and are unlikely to grow appreciably in the future.

Comparisons with Public School Lotteries

These three non-traditional methods finance educational extras – those highly specific undertakings which are peripheral to schools' core programs. Should state lotteries follow this lead? Should lottery funding – like user fees, enterprise activities, and foundation grants – be aimed at highly specific school activities and programs undertaken only sporadically and occasionally, when and if funds are available? That is, would the funding of highly specific school programs enable the average person to see the difference lottery funding makes? Is there, in the longer run, a surer and better method of school finance?

Taking user charges first, they reflect entirely the market principle. That is, user charges are a fee for services rendered. The child receives a service, say a field trip. The family pays its cost. In theory, at least, the field trip is voluntary; if it isn't worth the cost from the family's viewpoint the child won't go.

Lottery ticket buyers, on the other hand, receive no special school or other services based on their purchases. Nor would it seem possible to fashion a revenue system which turns lottery receipts into a user charge. If lotteries were to become user fees, they would have to finance some special government services that players receive and others don't. But players could not agree on which services to buy. Some lottery players don't have children and would not care about a school field trip. Some would prefer health care, and so forth. Lottery tickets are a chance a prize. Nothing else. They are in no way a user charge and the concept has no application to lotteries.

Could state lottery revenues fund an educational foundation? At first glance this seems an intriguing possibility, because it would seem to separate lottery finance from the state's legislative and budget-making processes. A non-government entity could be set up to fund educational projects.

But there is a problem. Legislators decide directly how to allocate the vast majority of school funds. And a central conclusion of this study has been: as soon as lottery revenues are mixed with other, larger revenue sources which support varied purposes, there is no way to assure that lotteries enhance public school funding. State legislatures could, and almost surely would, take into account the funding patterns of the state's lottery foundation in their school budgeting decisions. The public would still believe that schools are getting lottery money. Public officials would allocate funds with the view that the foundation was doing part of the job.

The lottery-sponsored public school foundation idea has substantial similarities to the proposal made earlier in this chapter for distributing lottery taxes very broadly among many charities. But in our view no one charity should be dependent on funds from this source. Certainly education should not become dependent on a lottery-financed foundation, even if funding authority is structurally separated from state government. The lottery foundation idea can be rejected as merely a cosmetic change.

Could lotteries be refashioned as enterprise activities, conducted expressly for and by the schools themselves? Could they become a form of revenue raising akin to bake sales and ticket sales for sports events?

Possibly. As discussed in Chapter 2, present laws restrict lottery operation to state government. If school districts or other local government entities were allowed to operate lotteries, the first step would be to change state laws. This seems remote, but not out of the question. As states enter more fully into casino gambling, they might turn over their lottery operations to local governments, including school districts. Hypothetically, at least, local schools might be empowered to run their own lotteries as enterprise activities, and so this alternative will have some appeal.

If state lotteries do not enhance public school funding as we contend, would local operation assure that the money gets to the schools? In a naive sense the answer is "yes." Viewed as an alternative for a school fair or a bake sale, a lottery might raise funds for, say, the purchase of computer software or junior prom decorations. In some settings schools have for years operated charity raffles, which are simply lotteries under another name.

Local school lotteries, conducted irregularly and for specific purposes marginal to the school's operation, may do no harm. Conceivably they may, in certain communities, build school commitment or awareness of the school's financial needs. But this is about the best that can be said of the practice. If local lotteries were to become a substantial and regular part of schools' operations, there is again the likelihood that local lottery revenues would substitute for local property taxes. Revenue substitution has occurred in the states. The same phenomenon would likely occur at the local level.

There would seem to be, in the long run, a far surer method of school revenue enhancement. That method is continued reliance on the regular tax system—income, sales, and property taxes. Assuming constant rates of tax, receipts from these sources grow about as fast as the economy grows.

It is widely acknowledged that, in the long run, the magnitude of school revenues depends on the economy. Schools are said to play a key role in promoting economic growth. The public and its elected representatives are currently fixated on the concept of growth. Reform proposals such as restructuring, national standards, and choice have economic growth as their ultimate aim. Yet states' methods of financing schools almost never directly reflect that aim. School funding decisions are viewed as short-term results of political compromise.

In the future, school funding should depend on a different principle—long-term economic growth. Such a change would connect political decisions about finance with the long-term well-being of the next generation. For example, if a state's economy were to grow at 3 percent per year for several years, the schools' budgets would grow at the same rate. The higher the state's economic growth, the greater the schools' budgetary increases. On the downside, if inflation were 4 percent in a year, and that state's real growth was only 3 percent, schools would suffer a loss in buying power in that particular year. This contrasts sharply with entitlement programs, where increases reflect inflation and not growth.

Under such a system, school finance decisions would reflect economic realities. Restructuring, national standards, school choice, etc., would still have unknown long-term effects. There would still be discussion and debate about their efficacy. But decisions about alternative school policies would be based on estimates of their productive merits, not mainly on short-term political considerations as is currently the case.

Nor would funding decisions rest on the vagaries of tax receipts in a particular year. States could use traditional taxes, new taxes, or even lotteries for some of their revenues if present policies persist. Schools would have the knowledge that their funding would not depend on one particular year's taxes.

There would be many objections to school funding based on long-term growth. Like many proposals based on simple principles, this one contains difficult complexities. A full discussion is well beyond the present scope. But hopefully the outlines of such a proposal given here will encourage fuller consideration.

A Role for Educational Leaders

If lottery revenues provided help for the public schools, educational leaders would have to weigh the problems lotteries raise against the benefit of enhanced funding. In fact, no such dilemma exists. Whatever their moral worth, lotteries do not help schools financially. Faced with this fact, education's leaders have three alternatives: they can be indifferent to lotteries, they can support lottery reforms trying to assure that the money reaches the schools, or they can actively oppose the claims of fiscal enhancement made by lottery proponents. The foregoing sections leave no doubt that the authors endorse the third position. However, alternatives one and two deserve consideration.

Indifference may be justified on the grounds that lottery games are seen to be professionally insignificant. It may be assumed that the education finance claims of lotteries are already known to be hyperbole. Professional opposition might confuse the voters, convincing them that schools don't need more money. Busy educators have more important things to worry about.

A central problem with indifference from the profession is that it leaves the issue wide open to the claims of outsiders—politicians, the gambling industry, and moralists. If educators don't participate in the lottery debate, who can be relied on to represent education's view? Educators may view moral claims for lotteries pro and con as a personal matter, but the financial claims manifestly are a concern to the profession.

The second alternative is restructuring the lottery to "truly" enhance public school finance. We have seen in Chapter 2 and the discussion immediately above, school or school district lotteries probably are legal under current federal laws. States could pass enabling legislation. The idea of local lotteries may be appealing to some people.

That local schools could raise revenue from lotteries we have no doubt. That lotteries would enhance local funding we view as most unlikely. The problems are exactly the same as those with state lotteries — earmarking and fungibility. Lottery revenues would simply replace local property taxes or state education aid, with no net gain. Local lotteries would have the same fiscal consequences as state lotteries.

This leaves our preferred (third) alternative: to actively work to inform the public that lotteries are not a solution to the problems of state finance. We argue that educators must actively reject false claims supposedly made on behalf of children. If we saw some product or service produced in the private market which falsely claimed to benefit children, we would think it our duty to object. The fact that lotteries are a state enterprise does not relieve us of our obligation.

CONCLUSION

This research is primarily descriptive. It aids in understanding the determinants of interstate variation in financial support and effort for the public schools. The study allows for only a coarse approach to understanding the possible impact of state lotteries on state support and effort for public schools. We provide a snapshot of the effects of the lottery at one point in time.

Schools are complex cultural institutions. Direct government intervention has only a limited role in affecting them in any profound way. On the other hand, lottery and school financial policy is impacted by interested parties. In our study, lottery variables are treated as discrete and independent. Nevertheless we have confidence in the results. Other studies using time series designs and well-settled economic theory confirm our main finding: modern state lotteries do not help schools.

Lotteries do contribute millions to elementary and secondary education. This is indisputable. But the lottery funds are used in place of other funding. Some work suggests that funds for basic programs are actually eroded overall as lottery revenues become the norm. If using lotteries for education does not result in significant fiscal enhancement, then lotteries produce no education benefits. This assumption has important implications for education policy. The gamble that lotteries actually would improve America's public schools or their funding is a gamble we can surely say is already lost.

Finance is discussed in conjunction with most public school improvement programs, such as restructuring, national standards, and choice. At best the lottery can only serve to divert attention from more substantive activities. At worst it can be harmful. Taxpayers and legislators may falsely assume that the lotteries and other gambling games can meet a substantial portion of public revenue needs. If so, the pressures to boost lottery sales or enact new gambling games will become more intense.

We think lottery operations reflect more deep-seated problems inherent in the contemporary state. To function in all the ways that modern governments must, requires high levels of affection and allegiance from the people. Lotteries are justified by their good works. Yet as lottery entrepreneur, the state risks those very affections and allegiances on which it relies for its good works. The state cannot be both the writer of the game's rules and the chief beneficiary of them. As a gambling entrepreneur, the state risks its role as moral agent. This is America's larger gamble. Is this the time for us to place a wager against the house?

Literature Review: Determinants of Educational Expenditure

A fundamental goal of social science is to understand the forces and their interactions which account for variation in policies and resource allocation among governmental units. Public expenditure theory evolved from a desire, on behalf of economists and political scientists, to understand why governments exhibit different patterns of expenditures for different public functions. The compelling need to understand the determinants of policies or expenditure patterns led to a concomitant desire to predict them.

In the 1960s several factors led to a rash of determinants studies. The availability of copious data from the U.S. Bureau of the Census was an important impetus. This proliferation of data coincided with modern developments in computer technology and statistical analysis. In addition, substantial increases in federal aid prompted policy analysts to perform more thorough assessments of the influence of grants, and to analyze expenditure needs relative to the fiscal capacity of states and cities. Finally, determinants studies resulted from an increased sensitivity to the importance of understanding why state and local government expenditures differ among jurisdictions.

Since a great proportion of public resources is devoted to financing public schools, economists often chose education as a function for analysis. Economists, therefore, preceded educators in investigating the determinants of education spending. Subsequently, with basic theory already in place, educational finance researchers tried to systematically isolate those aspects of economic development which have been responsible for the diverse character of our public education system.

Educators became particularly interested in determinants studies during the education reform period of the 1970s. During the reform years, courts began to equate per pupil expenditures with equal educational opportunity. With a better understanding of the conditions that influence school spending, the determinants of expenditure disparities became incorporated into state aid formulas, designed to distribute wealth and equalize "educational opportunity" among districts.

METHOD

Although some analyses of public expenditure patterns rely solely upon bivariate correlation (e.g., Berolzheimer, 1947; Dye, 1966, 1976), the predominant statistical technique in determinants studies is multivariate regression. Both cross-sectional and longitudinal designs have been developed, implicitly or explicitly, after models of consumer demand found in the private sector of the economy. Most determinants studies use a single equation, least squares method, with a district-level cross-sectional sample. However, state data of the type used in this effort were employed by Fabricant (1952), Renshaw (1960), Fisher (1961, 1964), Shapiro (1962), Sparkman (1977), Ohls and Wales (1972), Ryan (1985), and Strudwick (1985).

While there appears to be a general consensus with respect to basic method, no generally accepted theoretical paradigm has emerged from the innumerable determinants studies. The underlying lack of theory is reflected in the selection of disparate independent variables, units of observation, and data bases. For example, in many cases, factors are selected as predictors based upon the magnitude of their bivariate correlation with the dependent variable, rather than being dictated by hypotheses. Of course, the amount of variance a model can explain is related to the selection of particular independent variables.

This method of choosing independent variables according to the probability of increasing the coefficient of multiple determination, R^2, has been the topic of sharp criticism (Hirsch, 1960; McMahon, 1970; Morss, 1966; Strudwick, 1985). Critics object to the inherent lack of theory in this approach and stress that variable selection, to some degree, should be dependent on some theoretical rationale other than the possible maximization of R^2. As expenditure theory developed, some researchers began to demonstrate increased reliance upon explicit theoretical models which included rationales for most predictor variables (e.g., Barro, 1972; Hirsch, 1960; Ryan, 1985; Strudwick, 1985). These notwithstanding, the lack of underlying theory in much of the research remains the most important limitation of the determinants models.

Expenditures expressed in dollars are most frequently specified as the dependent variable. Spending may be expressed as combined state and local expenditures per capita, or for public education studies, expenditures per pupil. When the question is spending effort, expenditures are transformed into a unit government ratio of combined expenditures as a percentage of property values or personal income or as a ratio of expenditures to a balanced tax system (Sparkman, 1977; Advisory Commission on Intergovernmental Relations, 1989).

An economic approach would consider determinants of demand for education. Expenditures and revenues usually serve as a proxy for this measure. Since educational expenditures are not necessarily synonymous with educational output, some authors have attempted to measure quality or educational opportunity with such variables as pupil-teacher ratio, teacher salary, and achievement scores (e.g., Hirsch, 1960; Miner, 1963).

In the following section, some of the more notable determinants studies are discussed in a framework of broad categories of determinants. The discussion centers around how specific factors may be expected to influence demand or spending levels. The absence of a "best" model necessitates a careful examination of the literature so that an acceptable paradigm may be chosen or developed. An analysis of previous determinants studies facilitates the selection or modification of a model which minimizes theoretical and methodological weaknesses noted in the literature.

THE DETERMINANTS

Researchers have examined a wide range of variables to explain differences in expenditures and spending policies among states and localities. These variables may be classified into three major categories sketching a profile of the fifty states. Expenditure determinants studies assume that the policies and resultant expenditure levels of states and localities are products of these variables.

Measures of fiscal ability or wealth have been the most consistent and powerful determinants. The present lottery study uses state personal income as a general measure of a state's ability to finance education.

Community preference and cost variables, measured by social and demographic characteristics, have also been very effective in explaining and predicting educational spending. These variables reflect the assumption of possible demand and supply influences on educational spending levels (Ohls and Wales, 1972). The following community preference and cost variables have been included in this work: (1) population density, (2) urbanization, (3) the percentage of population which is school age, (4) schooling background of population, (5) the percentage of population that is non-white, and (6) private school enrollment.

The last general type refers to those variables that have governmental or political connotations. Political or governmental variables are assumed to have a direct influence on the decision-making process. They include factors such as geographical region, the legal status of school districts, type of school aid formula, party affiliation, type of administrative unit, the composition of school boards and administrative staffs, attitudes, and related forces (e.g., Crain and Rosenthal, 1967; Dye, 1966; Fredland et al., 1967; Morss, 1966; Rosenthal, 1980; Ryan, 1985; Zeigler and Johnson, 1972).

LOTTERY STATUS AS A POLITICAL VARIABLE

Most expenditure determinants models are constructed from socioeconomic and demographic variables. The relatively few studies that attempt to predict expenditure levels with political or attitudinal variables demonstrate the comparative weakness of these factors in explaining government spending. Zeigler and Johnson (1972), Sharkansky (1967), Hickrod (1971), and others showed that education expenditures share fewer relationships with political characteristics than does spending for other services. In the words of Hickrod (1971), "Overall, governmental factors have been a crashing disappointment." Dye (1977), Hofferbert (1968), and Zeigler and Johnson (1972) wrote that political variables are likely to yield misleading results when employed as predictors.

In an essay by Dye (1976), political scientists are reminded of their predispositions to rely on political and decision-making variables. Dye exhorted them to be flexible by looking beyond political forces, to economic ones, when attempting to explain public policy, especially fiscal policy. Dye contended that the associations between political forces and expenditures are mostly a result of the fact that economic development influences both political system characteristics and spending outcomes.

Jewell (1969) examined demand for education among heads of households. He used the desired level of property tax as a dependent variable. In interviews, subjects were told what "x" amount of tax would buy in terms of educational services. The important determinants were income, age, property tax paid, and attitude toward teachers' salaries. As expected, socioeconomic variables were much more powerful than political factors.

A study by Garms (1967) includes variables from administrative theory as possible predictors of education expenditures. The following factors failed to produce significant effects: (1) appointed versus elected school boards, (2) fiscal dependence versus fiscal independence, and (3) dual business manager/ superintendent administrative structure versus sole superintendent fiscal management.

In contrast, other works cite the theoretical and statistical importance of political variables in explaining expenditure patterns. Morehouse (1981) claimed that important political factors are often overshadowed by the statistically strong relationship between wealth and government spending. Zeigler and Johnson (1972) found that states with competitive, vigorous political parties tend to provide more educational aid. Rossmiller (1968) studied the effects of consensus on various matters of educational policy in Wisconsin. Rossmiller found that conflict seemed to have a stimulating effect on school expenditures, while consensus was inversely related to increasing demand for education. A similar variable, defined as "creative group conflict," was related to increases in demand for education in a study by Johns and Kimbrough (1968). In his final remarks about the relative influence and interaction among political and economic determinants, Lescault (1983) writes,

> Political determinants are the proximate causes of political outcomes. . . . Economic determinants however condition and influence political events. They provide the environment in which political decisions are made. Obviously then both economic and political determinants are important factors that are influential in predicting expenditures.

With the exception of the lottery variable—our prime focus—the determinants model in this research relies exclusively upon "classic" socioeconomic and demographic variables. One lottery variable (LOTED) takes the form of "lottery status" to identify those states that support public schools with lottery funds. A second lottery variable simply identifies a state on the basis of whether or not it operates a lottery. In this case lottery status can be more accurately ascribed to the political category.

TASTE AND COST VARIABLES

Socioeconomic and demographic variables are generally assumed to have an important influence on either the preferences of residents (consumers) or the costs of inputs within a jurisdiction. Urbanization (the percentage of people residing in SMSAs or standard metropolitan statistical areas) and population density (population per square mile) are among the first demographic variables found to be related to government spending. While the importance of these factors first became evident in the early works of Berolzheimer (1947) and Fabricant (1952), the significance of these demographic measures remains evident in more recent research. However, as is the case with most determinants, there is little consensus as to exactly how or to what extent these variables affect spending levels.

Berolzheimer suggested that the relationship between high expenditures and low population density may be due to diseconomies of scale, where fixed costs are prorated over a relatively small number of people or students. Axiomatically, this condition results in greater per unit costs. But if diseconomies of scale can result in higher costs in less populated states, how can one explain the higher expenditures incurred in densely populated areas? Since diseconomies of scale operate in areas of low population density, one would expect to see the effects of economies of scale (decreasing per unit costs) in cities and high density areas. Contrary to this expectation, Berolzheimer found education expenditures higher in cities and densely populated areas.

Berolzheimer offered two explanations for this phenomenon. First, teachers' salaries in these areas tend to be higher than average. A second reason is that urban areas usually have high enrollments. Berolzheimer seems to have omitted the widely held assumption that cities often incur higher expenses for goods and services (Jones, 1985).

The question of economies and diseconomies of scale reappears frequently in the literature. Hirsch (1960) predicted that the size of a jurisdiction will relate to expenditures in a parabolic manner. In simpler terms, he echoed Berolzheimer in the idea that educational expenditures will be higher for both very sparsely populated areas and for very densely populated areas.

Ryan (1985) found population density to be insignificant in predicting interstate variations in combined state-local education expenditures. But when he partitioned total spending into state aid and local components, he saw opposite relationships. In Ryan's analyses, the population density coefficient is positive for local expenditures and negative for state aid. According to him, the positive relationship suggested a preference for more public services and greater need for government outlay in urban areas. The inverse relationship suggests that densely populated states emphasize services other than education.

Ryan also noted that urbanization, or the percentage of a state's population residing in standard metropolitan statistical areas, is insignificant in predicting either total state-local spending, state aid, or local outlay. Like many other students of the problem, Ryan included urbanization and a measure of pupil density (the percentage of population which is school age) in the same models. He surmised that urbanization is not a significant predictor because the pupil density variable probably captures some of the same effects that metropolitan population is expected to capture.

Strudwick (1985) assumed that urbanization has a positive relationship with educational demand and preference, because of the greater employment opportunities of educated labor in urban areas. Strudwick and others also assumed that urban areas incur higher living, personnel, and building costs. On the other hand, Strudwick expected that population density lowers transportation costs, producing some degree of scale economies and lower expenditures per pupil. McMahon (1970) theorized that population density may affect expenditures by reducing inconvenience and private costs of travel.

Ohls and Wales (1972) held that urbanization, density, and other demographic variables do not significantly affect demand for education, but only the cost of the provision. They hypothesized that such variables affect state and local expenditures on education, not through the demand side of the market, but through the cost side. In their words,

> Variations in expenditures on education between relatively urban states and relatively rural states may be due, not to the fact that urban and rural citizens have different desires with respect to their children's schooling, but to the fact that the costs of providing given levels of education in the two settings are different.

Brazer (1959) explained 60 percent of the variation in the total per capita operating expenses of 462 cities with populations exceeding 25,000. Intergovernmental revenue, median family income, and population density were his best explainers. Brazer reported that these determinants of city spending, to a significant extent, could be used to explain spending in respective states. Brazer's contention has implications for this study. Although states, not cities, are the unit of analysis here, Brazer's variables would seem reasonable explainers of variation in school aid, expenditure, and effort to finance education.

Sacks and Ranney (1967) predicted 63 percent of the education expenses in selected urban areas. Their major determinants were per capita income, state aid, and school age population. Like Brazer, these researchers found that expenditures of central cities are affected by expenditures of surrounding areas. According to Sacks and Ranney, the association between higher expenditures and high-density states implies that, although high population densities lead to some technological efficiencies (economies of scale), more services are probably demanded in cities.

An important implication for this lottery study rests in the finding that unique factors peculiar to each state are the major determinants of spending. It is sometimes charged that state totals, like those used in this research, are often misleading because they mask intrastate disparities. The research of Brazer and Sacks and Ranney seems to contradict this assumption. It seems reasonable that the chances of obscuring intrastate disparities with aggregate statistics are decreased, to the extent that cities are characteristic of their respective states as a whole. Also, to the extent that the majority of a state's population resides in metropolitan areas, the determinants of city spending become synonymous with determinants of state spending.

Other social and demographic variables have been found to affect community preference or level of demand for education and other public functions. School age population, or the percentage of persons aged five to seventeen years, has been a significant and important determinant in many studies. But school age population or age reflects needs of specific groups, especially education of the young. McMahon (1970) concluded that larger percentages of school age populations lead to larger propensities to spend in lower income states, which tapers off in high income states where birth rates decline.

Public school substitutes, or the percentage of students enrolled in non-public schools in a given jurisdiction, are thought to form another dimension of community preference which impacts educational demand or expenditures. Fisher's 1961 study was probably the first to notice the possible influence of private school enrollment on public school spending. In his interstate study, Shapiro (1962) found private school enrollment insignificant in predicting educational expenditures. Ryan (1985) found state-local expenditures lower in states with higher percentages of private school enrollment. In Garms' 1967 study, private school enrollment was found to be a significant determinant of education expenditures. That study was done using a nationwide sample comprising 107 districts with enrollments exceeding 25,000 pupils.

McMahon reported that expenditure to income ratios fall in higher income states. McMahon attributed this decline to the larger proportion of children and the limited number of private schools which are often found in less wealthy jurisdictions. He added that the number of public school substitutes may indicate a lack of interest in schooling.

In a very comprehensive interstate determinants study, Strudwick (1985) recognized the opposing effects that high private school enrollments may have on per pupil expenditures. On the one hand it can be assumed, *ceteris paribus,* that larger percentages of private school students take a load off public education, thereby increasing revenue to be spent on each public pupil in that state. On the other hand, high private school enrollments may be indicative of an area's preference for high-quality education and will tend to be associated with increased school spending. Since the dominant effect is difficult to predict, any interpretation of this variable must recognize both possibilities.

The percent of state or city population that is non-white has been used to predict expenditures. Pidot (1969) pointed out that this variable may reflect differences in attitudes toward the role of the public sector in filling desires.

Shapiro's 1962 study explores factors that explain variation in education expenditures within regions of the United States. In that study the percent of non-white population is a significant determinant for the country as a whole, but it is not a good explainer of spending variation within regions of the country. Shapiro concluded that the percent of non-white population was serving as an indicator of regional trait complexes. The percentage of non-white population is related negatively to education expenditures in McMahon's (1970) work.

Strudwick (1985) hypothesized that non-white and schooling variables affect taste and demand for education via the effects of social conditions and discrimination in the labor and education markets. He assumed that states with high proportions of non-whites and illiterates are associated with low demand for education. It seems reasonable to assume that this effect may be strengthened by income effects, since non-white and illiteracy variables are closely and negatively associated with per capita income. Strudwick maintained, "These associations, rooted in poor fiscal ability, are likely to create a low demand for educational spending from states with relatively high proportions of non-whites and illiterates."

In summary, one can say that, conceptually, cost is an objective function. Indeed regional cost indices do exist. These indices, in turn, reflect differences in wealth (see discussion in the next section). Taste is more subjective — related to the lifestyles and social conditioning of individuals. Nevertheless, it has proven impossible to separate cost and taste variables through the public expenditure determinants literature reviewed here. Empirical measurement of this conceptual difference is an area worthy of further investigation in expenditure determinants research. Meanwhile the present research effort must live with the blur.

WEALTH

It is not surprising that most determinants studies conclude that measures of wealth are the best predictors of public expenditure. It is generally assumed that a process of modernization or economic development creates a set of circumstances that may facilitate passage of policies providing more public funds for particular services (Hofferbert, 1968).

In most studies, income is explicitly or implicitly chosen to represent this economic development. The early studies of Berolzheimer (1947) and Fabricant (1952) were the first in the literature to uncover the important, durable relationship between wealth and public expenditures. Shortly after World War II, Berolzheimer (1947) published three essays, wherein he introduced elements that led to the first determinants studies. Using data from the 1942 Census of Governments, he presented tabular analyses depicting relationships between state and local government expenditures and environmental factors which were later proven to be very durable determinants. He used indices of income, urbanization, and rural density with expenditures for education and other services. Berolzheimer found that higher income states generally had higher expenditures than lower income states.

Solomon Fabricant (1952), who is most often given credit for the first landmark study on expenditure determinants, found income to be the most important predictor of government spending. He was the first to employ multiple regression to analyze state disparities in combined state-local spending for all services, and state-local expenditures for selected public functions. Fabricant chose three environmental characteristics which Berolzheimer had discovered were related to public expenditures. Entering income, population density, and urbanization in a multiple regression model, Fabricant was able to explain 72 percent of combined state-local total expenditures. He used the same three predictor variables to explain between 29 percent (highways) and 85 percent (fire protection) of the variation in expenditures for other services. Fabricant's work became so widely acclaimed that his independent variables – income, population density, and urbanization – became known as the three "basic factors."

Fabricant's research has become the classic model for the "simple determinants school." It introduced enduring socioeconomic variables into a research design which is still used to predict and understand government expenditures (i.e., Ryan, 1985; Sparkman, 1977; Strudwick, 1985). These have been incorporated into the present study.

Subsequent studies conducted over the past thirty years reaffirm the importance of wealth or fiscal ability variables as the most consistent and powerful determinants of educational spending. Brazer (1959) explained 41 percent of variation in per capita current education expenses with median family income, average daily attendance, and state aid. Fisher (1961) found that property value and median family income were closely associated with interstate disparities in school spending. Sacks and Hellmuth (1961) studied school expenditures in thirty-two school districts in the Cleveland area. They claimed to explain 87 percent of the variance in current operating expenses with these variables: (1) Ohio intangible levy (a proxy for wealth), (2) state aid, and (3) assessed property valuation. State aid and property valuation allowed Sacks and Harris (1964) to account for 90 percent of the variation in school spending for fifty-eight counties in New York. James et al. (1966) predicted 77 percent of the variation in per pupil current operating expenses in 589 school districts in ten states. Their three major predictors were median family income, property valuations, and employment rate.

Hirsch (1960) examined determinants of public expenditures for public primary and secondary schools in twenty-nine school districts. He found per pupil assessed valuation to be the most powerful determinant. Since his quality indices did not have a high correlation with assessed valuation, he concluded that communities that can afford good education don't always provide it. He found the ratio of primary enrollment to secondary enrollment a significant predictor of school district spending. Miner (1963) had a similar finding with regard to the distribution of primary and secondary students.

As pointed out earlier, there is emphasis in the literature on the lack of theoretical specification in many determinants studies. In light of this caveat, the preceding review has focused on the hypothesized effects of the various wealth, taste and cost, and political variables on educational spending. Ostensibly, determinants researchers are far from achieving consensus on the consummate determinants paradigm of educational demand. Since this research attempts to minimize not only the theoretical but also the methodological problems that characterize interstate determinants studies, it is important to discuss a final aspect of public expenditure models.

CONCEPTUAL AND METHODOLOGICAL DILEMMAS

Although determinants studies are pervasive in economic and education finance literature, and serve as an acceptable model for this research, they are not without critics. Authors have highlighted at least two areas of inherent methodological weakness in many determinants models. These limitations are: (1) the multicollinearity among predictors, and (2) the questionable treatment of intergovernmental aid.

Bahl and Saunders (1966) were among the first who warned of the need to analyze the negating effects of multicollinearity in determinant studies. In a comprehensive work, McMahon (1970) reiterated concerns about the problem of multicollinearity and added that it is important to clarify the interrelation of determinants in both cross-sectional and longitudinal data. Kurnow (1963) also criticized the appropriateness of some linear regression models. He said that levels of basic variables are often interdependent. As an example, he asserted that the relationship between population density and educational expenditures is not independent of levels of income and urbanization.

While some determinants researchers have studied twenty to thirty variables simultaneously (e.g., Hofferbert, 1968; Pidot, 1969; Sergi, 1977; Sparkman, 1977), the problems of sample size and multicollinearity in the regression technique limit not only the choice but also the actual number of predictor variables that can be used to achieve interpretable results. Some researchers have looked to factor analysis in attempts to circumvent problems caused by the intercorrelation among and excess number of predictor variables.

Citing the problems of misleading high correlations and resultant poor parameter results, Pidot (1969) used factor analysis in an attempt to create unrelated measures and thereby avoid the multicollinearity dilemma. Without factor analysis, his regression results would have been difficult or impossible to interpret, given the number of variables (thirty) he wanted to test. He used the resultant factor scores in standard least squares regression. His six factors accounted for 50 to 70 percent of the variation in spending for most functions. Pidot maintained that factor analysis should also be performed, since the intercorrelation of independent variables may describe related dimensions of the same phenomenon. For example, property value correlates very highly with income, but may be considered a function of it.

Hofferbert (1968) also considered the possibility of the existence of major dimensions of socioeconomic structure within the states. In search of these dimensions, he performed factor analysis on twenty-one variables. Hofferbert hypothesized that if indicators of social structure are accurate, the intercorrelations and factor loadings should be stable in longitudinal analysis. To test his theory, he subjected his variables to factor analysis for each census year from 1890 to 1960. The statistical computation yielded two major factors. Hofferbert identified one factor as "industrialization," since it was defined by economic and employment variables. He referred to his second factor as "cultural enrichment." Educational attainment and the percent of non-white population loaded heavily on this factor. Hofferbert found the composition of these two major dimensions to be sufficiently stable over time. He held that this consistency allows one to consider them major enduring elements of social structure.

In an effort to decrease the number of potential independent variables and simultaneously increase R^2, Sparkman (1977) submitted twenty-eight variables to factor analysis. As Pidot had done, Sparkman used the resultant factor scores as independent variables in regression equations. He maintained that his selection of twenty-eight variables had been chosen from four broad classes which theretofore had been suggested in the literature. His wealth variables included measures such as per capita income, median family income, and percent of families below poverty level. Measures of urbanization, population density, percent of non-white population, percent of population in rural areas, and similar population data represented variables from the demographic category. Although they are considered by some to be of the demographic type, Sparkman used a group of variables that he perceived to comprise a broad category of public education. This group is represented by non–public school enrollment as a percent of total school enrollment, percent of public high school graduates, and percent of population aged twenty-five or older with less than five years of schooling.

Noting that public school finance falls within the framework of the total state economy, Sparkman identified a fourth category of variables that are related to governmental functions. The percent of school revenue from state government and the percent from the federal government would fall into this class. His four factors were able to explain less than 40 percent of the variance in two "effort for education" indices. Sparkman concluded that since so little of the variance in effort was explained, important factors must have been omitted from the original variable list. He suggested that future research focus on the possible interaction of political variables and socioeconomic variables.

Sparkman, Pidot, and Hofferbert made interesting and laudable attempts to deal with the ubiquitous problem of multicollinearity. However, two constraints limit the use of factor analysis techniques in this study. First, statisticians advise a minimum of six to ten observations (cases) for each variable

(Nunnally, 1978; Tabachnick and Fidell, 1983). Including the District of Columbia, the total cases in this study number fifty-one. With such an insufficient population size, the resultant factor structure would be questionable at best. There is a second reason that factor analysis is inappropriate in this work. Here we are interested in the effects of a specific variable, lottery. The possible influence of lotteries would be difficult or impossible to discern if they were expressed as part of a factor.

TREATMENT OF INTERGOVERNMENTAL REVENUE

The impact of intergovernmental funds is an important, recurring question in public expenditure literature. Many studies on the determinants of interstate spending variations have concerned the effects of state and federal grants, especially whether the effect of aid is stimulative or fungible. In order to reduce problems in interpretation, it is important to elucidate certain assumptions regarding the fiscal response issue. However, only limited aspects of this abiding issue are applicable to this effort.

One question that arises is whether state or federal aid should be among the list of predictor variables. When included, state aid has been an important predictor in approximately half of the interstate studies. Renshaw (1960), Bahl and Saunders (1966), Sacks and Harris (1964), and Ohls and Wales (1972) were among the researchers who concluded that state educational spending has substitutive effects on local spending.

Bishop examined the same question with somewhat different results. According to his results, state aid was more likely to have stimulative effects on school spending only in small districts. In addition, grant structure was as important as magnitude in determining local fiscal response. Ryan (1985) studied the extent to which recipient government expenditures may simultaneously affect donor government aid. His study concludes that the substitution effect of state aid on local expenditures is usually overestimated.

From a third perspective, Pogue and Sgontz (1968) said that state aid may be a function of local expenditures or may be determined, at least partially, by the same factors that determine them. These two researchers held that if state aid is determined by the same set of factors as local spending, state aid may not have stimulative effects, and it may be a proxy for other political and institutional variables. Gabler and Brest (1967) had a similar opinion with regard to state aid being a possible proxy for other determinants.

Since this effort examines both per pupil state aid and combined per pupil state-local expenditures, the possible substitutive or supplemental effects of state aid are accounted for. However, it would be inappropriate to include state aid as an independent variable in this model. Since state aid is a component of the criterion variables that represent support for education in this study, its inclusion as an independent variable would result in autocorrelation. Autocorrelation (or circularity), a major limitation in expenditure determinants models, is an extreme example of multicollinearity where a dependent variable is regressed on itself or a large component thereof.

Researchers have also considered the influence of federal transfers. According to Sacks and Harris (1964) and Bahl and Saunders (1966), federal aid increases explained spending variation significantly. In a related finding, Adams (1965) concluded that intergovernmental aid was more substitutive in less developed regions of the country. He also found that measures of effort were influenced by state and federal aid.

Morss (1966) and Fisher (1964) stress that the objectives of an expenditure study should determine the research methods. Knowing that expenditures increase with federal aid (especially when states must spend all of the outside money) is, according to Morss, "hardly an interesting finding" and contributes little to the understanding of fiscal behavior.

In this work, the inclusion of federal aid would introduce an element of circularity without adding to the understanding of how lotteries may influence interstate differences in the education provision. As Bahl (1969) notes, "It is not surprising that if all other things are held constant, higher levels of grants are associated with higher levels of expenditures."

Hence, this study uses expenditures from own sources as the dependent variable and omits federal intergovernmental aid as a possible determinant. For the purposes of this study, a basic assumption is that education revenues are derived solely from jurisdictional sources. Given the limitations inherent in using aggregate state data, it seems that the inclusion of federal aid would unnecessarily cloud the possible influence of the lottery in explaining interstate differences. We acknowledge that there is a good deal of variation in the types of revenue that make up own sources across states. To an undetermined extent, this study is designed specifically to test for differences in state and local spending due to differences in revenue policies, particularly lotteries.

The preceding literature review sketched the major developments in public expenditure theory and outlined various issues and approaches taken in determinants studies. This treatment of the literature provided a theoretical underpinning, and helped establish justification for the basic model used to study lotteries as a determinant of support for education among the states.

THE MODEL

Most of the studies discussed in the foregoing review fall into a category that Strudwick (1985) identified as "the simple determinants school." Here, works are characterized by a lack of explicit theory. These efforts are based on the assumption that statistical significance must have underlying causal relationships.

In what is the most comprehensive and up-to-date investigation of its kind, Strudwick (1985) analyzed the determinants of interstate educational spending over a 100-year period, 1870 to 1970. He reiterated many of the weaknesses of former studies and addressed methods, techniques, and assumptions he employed to avoid previous dilemmas. Because of its cross-sectional design, and the intuitive appeal of the theoretical underpinnings, this paradigm was chosen as the operational model for this work. Strudwick's model has the following features.

(1) It places emphasis on government officials as the prime factors in determining levels of educational expenditure.

(2) It assumes that policy or spending decisions are determined primarily by politicians and government officials. This particular tenet is applicable to the case of state lotteries. Surely, success or failure of lottery legislation and the tenuous relationship between lotteries and levels of educational provision are, to a great extent, functions of political behavior.

(3) It uses a relatively simple estimating equation, facilitating estimation and interpretive potential. Strudwick's model has been adapted to serve as a benchmark for the addition of a lottery variable.

Application of this model is discussed in Chapter 4 and Appendix B.

Definition of Terms, Research Questions, and Hypotheses

IN order to determine accurately the relationship between fiscal policy (lotteries) and support for education, specific operational definitions must be selected or developed. While there is consensus with respect to the measurement of lottery funds, the meaning of the term "support for education" varies according to the purposes and assumptions of the researcher.

In this study, support for education (ISEE) is operationally defined according to four indices: two direct expenditure indices, and two effort measures.

EDUCATION EXPENDITURES

When making comparisons among and between governmental units, educators, officials, and organizations such as the National Education Association, the Education Commission of the States, and the U.S. Department of Education, report both education revenues and expenditures. However, since states with larger enrollments will necessarily spend greater total amounts on public schools than smaller states, total amounts are usually divided by some form of enrollment figure (educational load) and reported as revenue or expenditure per pupil. Obviously, this numerical transformation facilitates data comparisons. The literature suggests that analysis of revenues or expenditures can be expected to yield similar results in a determinants model using aggregate state data (Strudwick, 1985). Nevertheless, this study uses expenditures as a measure of the direct fiscal support a state provides for its public schools K–12. Two expenditure statistics are employed: (1) per pupil state aid in average daily attendance (ADA), and (2) per pupil state-local expenditures (from state and local sources) in average daily attendance (National Education Association, 1988b; U.S. Bureau of the Census, 1988b).

Per Pupil State Aid (SA)

This magnitude measure represents the amount of money a state allocates for elementary and secondary education K–12. State aid is a logical dependent variable in this study for two reasons. The unit of analysis is the state, and state governments now provide the financing for the major share of school support (National Education Association, 1988a). Secondly, lottery revenues are collected and distributed at the state level. Where applicable, this measure reflects lottery funds that are earmarked for schools and those that are distributed as school aid through the state general fund. The major components of this measure, however, vary according to the tax structure of the state.

While income and sales taxes are the major sources of state revenue nationwide, it is important to point out that as of 1987, approximately nine states did not have a major income tax and five states did not levy a sales tax. New Hampshire and Alaska have neither tax (Advisory Commission on Intergovernmental Relations, 1987). In states with this limited taxation, liquor, motor fuel, tobacco, and miscellaneous state taxes and charges comprise a greater portion of intergovernmental revenues from states to localities; of course the relative significance of lotteries may be greater in these states.

Per Pupil State-Local Expenditures (SL)

States also provide general aid to cities and towns, which can be used as a discretionary fund by the lower levels of government. Such funds may be reflected in local education expenditures, but may not necessarily appear as state education aid. In states where lottery profits become part of the general fund, school expenditures at the local level may reflect state education aid that is not reported as such by the state. In Massachusetts, for example, lottery funds are earmarked for general aid to cities and towns. The measure, SL, attempts to capture the effects of this general aid, which is ultimately used for public schools.

This inclusive measure is also chosen because it has been demonstrated that state aid may have a stimulative effect on local education spending (Ryan, 1985). Here, the rationale is that as states provide more lottery revenue in the form of education aid to local governments, local school districts may themselves spend greater amounts than they would have without the addition of lottery revenue. Although some researchers have found federal aid to have a stimulative effect on state-local expenditures, aid from the federal government is excluded from analysis in this study. The focus of this thesis is on interstate differences in education spending as a possible result of lottery revenues raised within individual states. Hence, federal aid is viewed as a superfluous, possibly confounding element.

There is still another reason for the inclusion of state-local expenditures. The dollar amount and percentage of state aid may be related more to historical, regional, and political variables that have been in operation for many years (Strudwick, 1985). Hence, an examination of state aid may not be very sensitive to increases from the lottery in those states where relatively small percentages of total school revenues have originated at the state level. Since this is a cross-sectional study, changes in patterns of revenue will not be examined over time. In addition, interstate variations in total school spending from state sources is the primary concern of this study. It has been shown that total school spending is related to socioeconomic conditions within a state or district.

EFFORT FOR EDUCATION

Since the ability of governments to support public education depends on economic development, natural resources, and other environmental factors, collectors and users of education finance data attempt to look beyond absolute dollar amounts. Although revenues per pupil indicate the fiscal magnitude of a state's educational provisions, these statistics do not reveal the relative effort the jurisdiction must make to maintain a particular level of support. Therefore, researchers and policy analysts are interested in measuring "effort" indices, which reflect the percentage relationship between educational revenues or expenditures, and some measure of tax capacity (Johns et al., 1983). Derivatives of this concept are integral components of state and federal aid formulas.

In this work, two alternative measures of state effort for education are selected. One is based on the concept described above, and considers expenditures as a percent of capacity. The other examines state governments' expenditures on public schools (state aid) relative to expenditures for other functions. According to Lescault (1983), both measures tend to neutralize possible effects of interstate variation in the cost of living.

State Aid as a Percent of State Government Expenditures (SAEFI)

This index is a measure of the state effort in education relative to other state efforts. This measure is not directly affected by economic development because wealthy, urban, industrial states simply spend more for all public functions (Dye, 1966). This measure is computed by dividing the total amount of elementary and secondary state school aid to cities, towns, and school districts by total general state government general expenditures.

State-Local Expenditures as a Percent of State Personal Income (SLEF2)

The relationship between income and public spending has long been established. Thus, income is considered to be an accurate measure of ability to finance education. This measure holds constant for a state's ability to spend and, to a degree, measures a state's willingness to sacrifice personal income for public education (Dye, 1972). This indicator is derived by dividing per pupil state-local education expenditures (SL) by net personal income in 1987 per pupil in ADA. Income affects ability to spend at both the state and local levels. This effort index reflects total education expenditures from state and local sources (excluding federal aid) as a portion of the income behind each pupil in average daily attendance.

Lottery Variables

There are two types of lottery variables employed in this study. The categories are developed according to three possible methods of measuring the influence of state lotteries on interstate variation in education spending.

(1) Lottery (L): this is a dichotomous variable that simply identifies each state as a "lottery state" ($n = 23$) or a "non-lottery state" ($n = 28$) in 1987. This dichotomy helps determine whether states that have implemented lotteries share similar socioeconomic or demographic characteristics.

(2) Lottery for Education (LOTED): this discrete dichotomous variable categorizes all states into two groups: (1) states which claim that their lotteries enhance support for public education K–12, and (2) states which either do not have lotteries or whose lotteries are mainly used to fund other public functions. Where the lottery variable (L) facilitates investigation into the determinants of state lottery status, LOTED enables us to address a more specific question of whether or not those states that implement lotteries for the sake of schools, demonstrate greater support or effort than non-lottery states or states that use lottery profits for other functions.

Socioeconomic and Demographic Variables

Many researchers have studied the relationship between socioeconomic and demographic characteristics and variations in educational spending among jurisdictions. The variables that emerge from the theoretical discussions in Chapter 2 and Chapter 4 are thought to reflect the influence of cost and supply forces and the tastes of residents. In pure economic terms, the variables below generally serve as proxies for major factors which are assumed to affect demand for education.

(1) Per Capita Personal Income (PCI): the aggregate or total state income received by persons residing in a state divided by the total state population. This is shown to have a significant effect on the financial resources available to governmental jurisdictions through taxation. It is a gauge of the ability to generate funds for public programs (National Education Association, 1988a).

(2) Percent State Population which is Non-White (PNWT): the percentage of state residents who are classified by the U.S. Bureau of the Census as being any other race but Caucasian. PNWT includes residents who are Black, American Indian, Eskimo, Asian, and Pacific Islander (U.S. Bureau of the Census, 1986).

(3) Population Density (PSQM): total state land area in square miles divided by the total resident population (U.S. Bureau of the Census, 1987).

(4) Private School Enrollment (PVSE): percentage of total pupils, grades one to twelve, enrolled in non-public schools (U.S. Department of Education, 1987).

(5) Percent of Population which is School Age (SAP): percentage of state residents age five to seventeen, excluding armed forces abroad (National Education Association, 1988a).

(6) Percent of Urban Population (URB): percentage of people living in places of 2,500 or more inhabitants, or other locations designated as urban by the U.S. Bureau of the Census (U.S. Bureau of the Census, 1987).

(7) School Background of the Population (PPHS): percentage of population twenty-five years and older who have completed at least four years of high school (U.S. Bureau of the Census, 1982).

THE MODEL

Our model incorporates the variables above in the following generalized form. Conceptually, the equation is written as follows:

School Expenditures and Support	= (f)	Social Variables	+	Economic Variables	+	Demographic Variables	+	Political Variables
SA		PVSE		PCI		PNWT		L
SL		SAP				PSQM		LOTED
SAEF1		PPHS						
SLEF2								

where

f = a mathematical function weighting of each predictor variable to determine that variable's importance in predicting the dependent variable

SA = state school aid per pupil

SL = state-local school expenditures per pupil

SAEF1 = state school aid as a percent of all government expenditures

SLEF2 = state school aid as a percent of personal income

PVSE = private school enrollments as a percentage of total enrollments

SAP = percentage of the population which is school age

PPHS = percentage of the population which has at least a high school diploma

PCI = income per capita

L = "lottery," a dichotomous variable denoting the presence or absence of a lottery in each state

LOTED = a dichotomous variable indicating whether a statute exists earmarking lottery revenues for schools

PNWT = percentage of the population which is non-white

PSQM = population density

HYPOTHESES AND STATISTICAL PROCEDURES

The process of rejecting or failing to reject the null hypotheses below is accomplished by employing three major statistical procedures. This section discusses the statistical methods that were used to test each of the fourteen hypotheses. A discussion of each procedure is introduced by its respective hypotheses. In Chapter 4, the term "support for education" was operationally defined according to four different variables: two expenditure indices and two effort measures. To facilitate explanation of the analyses, these four criterion variables are treated separately and are not collapsed into groups of research questions as they were in Chapter 4.

- Hypothesis one: there is no significant relationship between per pupil state aid and selected state socioeconomic and demographic characteristics.
- Hypothesis two: there is no significant relationship between per pupil state-local expenditures and selected socioeconomic and demographic characteristics.
- Hypothesis three: there is no significant relationship between state aid

as a percent of state government expenditures and selected socioeconomic and demographic characteristics.

- Hypothesis four: there is no significant relationship between state-local expenditures as a percent of personal income and selected socioeconomic and demographic characteristics.

These four hypotheses established a timely, relevant base of determinants to which the lottery variable could be compared. The socioeconomic and demographic statistics specified in the equation above were entered as independent variables in stepwise multiple regression. Each hypothesis used a different indicator of support and effort for education as the dependent variable.

Multiple regression is the statistical technique used in most expenditure determinants research. It seeks to establish a relationship between explanatory or "independent variables" and the object of the explanation, "dependent variables." In the education case, school spending is the variable to be explained. Social context variables specifically related to education do the explaining. The relationship takes the form of a mathematical equation. On the other side are the myriad of social, political, demographic, and economic factors — the independent variables, which conceivably might be combined to explain variation in school revenues or expenditures.

- Hypothesis five: after adjusting for the effects of the major determinants, there is no significant relationship between per pupil state aid and state lottery use.
- Hypothesis six: after adjusting for the effects of the major determinants, there is no significant relationship between per pupil state-local expenditures and state lottery use.
- Hypothesis seven: after adjusting for the effects of the major determinants, there is no significant relationship between state aid as a percent of state government expenditures and state lottery use.
- Hypothesis eight: after adjusting for the effects of the major determinants, there is no significant relationship between state-local expenditures as a percent of personal income and state lottery use.

Hierarchical multiple regression was used to test the preceding four hypotheses. The lottery uses variable was forced into each equation after the stepwise procedures had been run. The amount of explained variance in each equation (hypothesis one to hypothesis four) was compared with the amount of explained variance in each of the matching measures of support and effort in equations (hypothesis five to hypothesis eight).

- Hypothesis nine: there is no significant difference between states which purport to use lottery revenues to fund public education and states which do not with respect to their per pupil state aid.

- Hypothesis ten: there is no significant difference between states which purport to use lottery revenues to fund public education and states which do not with respect to per pupil state-local education expenditures.
- Hypothesis eleven: there is no significant difference between states which purport to use lottery revenues to fund public education and states which do not with respect to state aid as a percent of state government expenditures.
- Hypothesis twelve: there is no significant difference between states which purport to use lottery revenues to fund public education and states which do not with respect to per pupil state-local expenditures as a percent of personal income per pupil.

Null hypotheses nine to twelve were tested through four t-tests. One t-test was run for each measure of educational support and effort. Attendance, not membership, was used as the per pupil measure throughout the study.

- Hypothesis thirteen: there is no significant relationship between the lottery status of states and selected socioeconomic and demographic variables.
- Hypothesis fourteen: there is no significant relationship between states which purport to use lottery revenues to fund public education and selected socioeconomic and demographic variables.

Hypotheses thirteen and fourteen were tested using multiple regression. In null hypothesis thirteen, the state's lottery status was the dependent variable (L). States that operated a lottery in 1987 were assigned a value of "1" for L; all other states were assigned "2." The independent variables were the socioeconomic and demographic measures from the determinants model discussed above and in Chapter 4. The lottery-for-education variable (LOTED) was treated as dichotomous and dependent in null hypothesis fourteen. States which claimed that the lottery enhanced public school funding in 1987 were assigned the value of "1" for the LOTED variable; where there was no lottery, or where lottery revenues were used to support other state programs, the value of "2" was assigned. The same set of socioeconomic and demographic characteristics were used as predictors in each procedure.

To minimize conceptual and methodological weaknesses inherent in some public expenditure studies, a specific determinants model is carefully chosen. A rationale is provided for each of the independent variables. The inclusion of specific predictor variables is based on their theoretical influence on interstate variation in support for public schools. Since the state is the unit of analysis, a total population of fifty-one (including the District of Columbia) necessitates guarded selection of these independent variables. Incorporation of other less justifiable predictors into the determinants model could maximize R^2 but compromise the theoretical integrity of the study. As discussed in Chapter 2, some determinants studies have included variables that automatically result in very high R^2 values but violate sound theoretical and methodological practice.

Our model for inclusion of lottery revenues in "fiscal determinants" studies is presented in Chapter 4 and elaborated in the literature review in Appendix A. The maximization of R^2 is not the prime focus of this study. The initial stepwise regression procedures are crucial in that they establish benchmarks to which the introduction of LOTED may be compared.

LIMITATIONS

Since this is a cross-sectional correlational study, any relationships between the predictor and criterion variables cannot be interpreted as being causal. In testing the hypotheses, type one errors may have resulted because of the inherent lack of control in this *ex post facto* research.

This study is limited to a select group of socioeconomic and demographic variables which, according to the literature (e.g., Fabricant, 1952; Miner, 1963; Ryan, 1985; Sparkman, 1977; Strudwick, 1985; Zeigler and Johnson, 1972), is related to differences in educational funding among governmental units. Factors beyond the scope of this study may be important determinants of support for education, and may also be significantly related to the lottery status of individual states. Extraneous variables such as political climate and political affiliation are threats to internal validity. Problems of multicollinearity of the predictor variables are considered too important to be relegated to an appendix. These are discussed in Chapters 4 and 5.

BIBLIOGRAPHY

ADAMS, R. F. 1965. "On the Variation in the Consumption of Public Services," *Review of Economics and Statistics*, 47:400–405.

ADVISORY COMMISSION ON INTERGOVERNMENTAL RELATIONS. 1987. *Significant Features of Fiscal Federalism: 1987 Edition.* Washington, DC: U.S. Government Printing Office.

ADVISORY COMMISSION ON INTERGOVERNMENTAL RELATIONS. 1989. *1987 State Fiscal Capacity and Effort.* Washington, DC: U.S. Government Printing Office.

ADVISORY COMMISSION ON INTERGOVERNMENTAL RELATIONS. 1991. *Significant Features of Fiscal Federalism, Volume 2, Revenues and Expenditures.* Washington, DC: U.S. Government Printing Office.

ALLEN, P. J. 1991. "The Allocation of Lottery Revenues to Education in Florida, California, Michigan and Illinois," *Educational Policy,* 5(3):296–311.

AMALFITANO, J. L. 1989. "The Relationship between Lotteries and Support for Education among the States," unpublished Ph.D. dissertation, University of Connecticut, Storrs, CT.

AMALFITANO, J. L. AND T. H. Jones. 1990. "The Relationship between Lotteries and Support for Education among the States," paper presented at the *Annual Conference of the American Educational Finance Association*, Las Vegas, NV.

AMES, S. B. 1987. "Addiction Risk Linked to Lottery," *The Oregonian* (February 1):11.

ANON. 1987. "Are Lotteries Really the Ticket?" *New York Times* (January 4):14.

ANON. 1975. "Economic Case Against State-Run Gambling," *Business Week* (August 4):67–68.

ANON. 1988. "The Electorate of North Dakota," *Gaming and Wagering Business,* 9(12):14.

ANON. 1988. "Gamble and Be Taxed," *The Economist,* 306(January 16):78.

ANON. 1991. "Gross Annual Wager," *Gaming and Wagering Business,* 12(7):32–33.

ANON. 1989. "Kentucky Creates Unique Corporate Structured Lottery, a la Canada," *Gaming and Wagering Business* (January):10.

175

ANON. 1991. "Leisure Time Industry," *Industry Surveys*. New York, NY: Standard and Poor's Corp. (July):L21.

ANON. 1991. "Lotteries Abroad," *Gaming and Wagering Business*, 12(5):19.

ANON. 1988. "Lotteries a Great Deal for States—But Not So Great for the Players," *The Providence Sunday Journal* (August 28):F-6.

ANON. 1988. "Lottery Agents Claim Nearly $1 Billion in 1988," *Gaming and Wagering Business* (November 15):16–20.

ANON. 1974. "Lottery's Not the Best Bet as Tax Aid, Majority Feels," *The Hartford Times* (April 10):1.

ANON. 1988. "Many States Find Lotteries Are Dangerous Social Gamble," *The Providence Journal* (July 24):A-1.

ANON. 1988. "NJ Lottery to Post Hotline Number," *Gaming and Wagering Business* (September 15):46.

ANON. 1990. "On a Roll, Gambling in the United States," *The Economist*, 314(January 20):29.

ANON. 1986. *SPSSX User's Guide, 2nd Edition*. New York, NY: McGraw-Hill Book Co.

ANON. 1974. "State Lotteries: A Legal Sucker Bet," *Consumer Reports* (February):177–179.

ANON. 1988. "U.S. Lottery Ad Costs Soar," *Gaming and Wagering Business* (September 15):32–38.

ANON. 1988. "Va. Lottery Seeks Bill to Allow Info Blackout," *Gaming and Wagering Business* (October 15):60.

ANON. 1991. "Which States Have Which Games," *Gaming and Wagering Business*, 12(8):18–20.

ARIZONA STATE LOTTERY. 1988. *Annual Report 1987*. Phoenix, AZ.

ARNOLD, R. 1987. *Los Angeles Times* (January 4):1–2.

ARONSON, J. R. AND E. SCHWARTZ, eds. 1981. *Management Policies in Local Government Finance*. Washington, DC: International City Management Association.

ARONSON, J. R., A. WEINTRAUB, AND C. WALSH. 1972. "Revenue Potential of State and Local Lotteries," *Growth and Change* (April):3–8.

ASHTON, J. C. 1898. *The History of Gambling in England*. London: Duckworth.

ASSOCIATED PRESS. 1989. "Wagers Race to Illinois for Shot at $67 Million," *Providence Sunday Journal* (April 17):A-2.

BAHL, R. W. 1969. "Studies on Determinants of Public Expenditures: A Review," in *Sharing Federal Funds for State and Local Needs*, S. J. Mushkin and J. Cotton, eds., New York, NY: Praeger, pp. 185–203.

BAHL, R. W. 1970. "Quantitative Public Expenditure Analysis and Public Policy," in *National Tax Association, Proceedings of the Sixty-Second Annual Conference on Taxation*, p. 548.

BAHL, R. W. AND R. J. SAUNDERS. 1966. "Fabricant's Determinants after Twenty Years: A Critical Reappraisal," *American Economist*, 10:27–42.

BARRO, S. M. 1972. *An Econometric Study of Public School Expenditure Variations across States, 1951–1967*. Santa Monica, CA: Rand Corporation, p. 4934.

BATCH, R. 1987. "What Should Lottery Legislation Contain?" in *Handbook of U.S.*

Lottery Fundamentals, D. L. Hancock, ed., Washington, DC: Public Gaming Research Institute, pp. 52–53.

BELL, R. C. 1976. "Moral Views on Gambling Promulgated by Major Religious Bodies," in *Gambling in America, Interim Report.* Springfield, VA: National Technical Information Service, U.S. Department of Commerce. Accession No. 243817/Y3. G14 2R7.

BEROLZHEIMER, J. 1947. "Influences Shaping Expenditure for Operations of State and Local Governments," *Bulletin of the National Tax Association,* 32:170–171, 213–219, 237–244.

BERRY, F. S. 1987. "Tax Policy Innovation in the American States," Ph.D. dissertation, University of Minnesota.

BIRD, E. T. 1972. "State Lotteries—A Good Bet," *State Government* (Winter).

BLAKEY, G. R. 1979. "State Conducted Lotteries: History, Problems, and Promises," *Journal of Social Issues,* 35:62–86.

BORG, M. O. AND P. M. MASON. 1987. "The Budgetary Incidence of a Lottery to Support Education," *National Tax Journal,* 41:75–86.

BORG, M. O. AND P. M. MASON. 1990. "Earmarked Lottery Revenues: Positive Windfalls or Concealed Redistribution Mechanisms?" *Journal of Education Finance,* 15(3):298–301.

BOSANQUET, N. 1983. *Economics after the New Right.* Boston, MA: Kluwer-Nijhoff Academic Publishers Group.

BRAZER, H. E. 1959. *City Expenditures in the United States.* New York, NY: National Bureau of Economic Research.

BRENNER, R. AND G. BRENNER. 1990. *Gambling and Speculation.* Cambridge, England: Cambridge University Press.

BRINNER, R. E. AND C. T. CLOTFELTER. 1975. "An Economic Appraisal of State Lotteries," *National Tax Journal,* 28:397.

BYARD, K. 1987. "Lottery Profits Have Circular Route," *Akron Beacon Journal* (March 25).

CALIFORNIA STATE LOTTERY. 1988. *Annual Report 1987.* Sacramento, CA.

CAMPBELL, D. T. AND J. C. STANLEY. 1963. *Experimental and Quasi-Experimental Designs for Research.* Boston, MA: Houghton-Mifflin.

CELIS, W. 1991. "Florida Looks to Lottery to Ease Education Cuts," *New York Times* (February 27):88.

CLOTFELTER, C. T. 1979. "On the Regressivity of State-Operated Numbers Games," *National Tax Journal,* 32:543–548.

CLOTFELTER, C. T. AND P. J. COOK. 1987. "Implicit Taxation in Lottery Finance," *National Tax Journal,* 15:533–546.

CLOTFELTER, C. T. AND P. J. COOK. 1989. *Selling Hope,* Cambridge, MA: Harvard University Press.

CLOTFELTER, C. T. AND P. J. COOK. 1990. "Redefining Success in the State Lottery Business," *Journal of Policy Analysis and Management,* 9(1):99–104.

COLORADO STATE LOTTERY. 1988. *Annual Report 1987.* Denver, CO.

COLSON, C. 1987. "The Myth of the Money Tree," *Christianity Today,* 31(July 10):64.

COMMISSION ON THE REVIEW OF THE NATIONAL POLICY TOWARD GAMBLING. 1975. *First Interim Report.* Washington, DC: U.S. Government Printing Office.

COMMISSION ON THE REVIEW OF THE NATIONAL POLICY TOWARD GAMBLING. 1976. *Gambling in America.* Washington, DC: U.S. Government Printing Office.

CONNECTICUT STATE LOTTERY. 1988. *Annual Report 1987.* Newington, CT.

CRAIN, R. AND A. ROSENTHAL. 1967. "Community Status as a Dimension of Local Decision Making," *American Sociology Review,* 32:983–994.

DAYTON, J. AND M. MCCARTHY, 1992. "User Fees in Public Schools: Are They Legal?" *Journal of Education Finance,* 18(2):127–141.

DELAWARE STATE LOTTERY. 1988. *Annual Report 1987.* Dover, DE.

DENZEAU, A. T. 1975. "An Empirical Survey of Studies of Public School Spending," *National Tax Journal,* 28:241–248.

DEPARTMENT OF COMMERCE, BUREAU OF THE CENSUS. 1991. *Statistical Abstract of the United States, 1991.* Washington, DC: U.S. Government Printing Office, p. 280.

DEVEREUX, E. C., JR. 1980. *Gambling and the Social Structure.* New York, NY: Arno Press.

DISTRICT OF COLUMBIA LOTTERY. 1988. *Annual Report 1987.* Washington, DC.

DONLAN, T. G. 1991. "The War Between the States," *Barrons* (October 7):10.

DYE, T. R. 1966. *Politics, Economics, and the Public: Policy Outcomes in the American States.* Chicago, IL: Rand McNally.

DYE, T. R. 1972. *Understanding Public Policy.* Englewood Cliffs, NJ: Prentice-Hall.

DYE, T. R. 1976. *Policy Analysis: What Governments Do, Why They Do It, and What Difference It Makes.* Tuscaloosa, AL: University of Alabama Press.

DYE, T. R. 1977. *Politics in States and Communities.* Englewood Cliffs, NJ: Prentice-Hall.

DYE, T. R. AND V. GRAY. 1980. *The Determinants of Public Policy.* Lexington, MA: D. C. Heath and Company.

EADINGTON, W. 1984. "The Casino Gaming Industry: A Study in Political Economy," *The Annals of the American Academy of Social and Political Sciences,* 474:23–35.

ELAZAR, D. 1972. *American Federalism: A View from the States.* New York, NY: Thomas Y. Crowell Co.

ELLIS, V. 1990. "Lottery Sales Slump Will Reduce Share to Education," *Los Angeles Times* (December 8):A37.

EZELL, J. S. 1960. *Fortune's Merry Wheel: The Lottery in America.* Cambridge, MA: Harvard University Press.

FABRICANT, S. 1952. *The Trend of Government Activity in the United States Since 1900.* New York, NY: National Bureau of Economic Research.

FABRICIUS, M. A. AND R. K. SNELL. 1990. *Earmarking State Taxes.* Denver, CO: The National Conference of State Legislatures.

FARNEY, D. 1986. "More States Bet on Lotteries to Increase Revenue as Popularity of This 'Painless Taxation' Grows," *Wall Street Journal* (February 6):42.

FILER, J. E., D. L. MOAK, AND B. UZE. 1988. "Why Some States Adopt Lotteries and Others Don't," *Public Finance Quarterly,* 16(3):259–283.

FISHER, G. W. 1961. "Determinants of State and Local Government Expenditures: A Preliminary Analysis," *National Tax Journal,* 14:349–355.

FISHER, G. W. 1964. "Interstate Variation in State and Local Government Expenditures, *National Tax Journal,* 17:55–74.

FITZGERALD, J. F. 1989. "Lotteries, Bureaucrats Don't Mix, Says Lewis," *The Hartford Courant* (June 8):A22.

FLORIDA SENATE, SELECT COMMITTEE ON THE LOTTERY. 1987. *Final Report.* Tallahassee, FL: State of Florida.

FREDLAND, J. E., S. HYMANS, AND E. MORSS. 1967. "Fluctuations in State Expenditures: An Economic Analysis, *Southern Economic Journal,* 33:496–517.

FREY, J. H. 1984. "Gambling: A Sociological Review," *The Annals of the American Academy of Political and Social Science,* 474:91–106.

GABLER, L. R. AND J. I. BREST. 1967. Interstate Variations in Per Capita Highway Expenditures," *National Tax Journal,* 20(1):78–85.

GARMS, W. I. 1967. "Financial Characteristics and Problems of Large City School Districts," *Educational Administration Quarterly,* 3:14–27.

GOLD, S. D. 1990. "The Effect of Earmarked Revenue on State Spending for Schools," paper presented to the *American Educational Finance Association,* Las Vegas, NV, March 15–17.

GOLD, S. D. ET AL. 1990. *Earmarking State Taxes.* Denver, CO: The National Conference of State Legislatures.

GREENFIELD, E. 1991. "New Trends in . . . At-Risk and Special Education Products: Tools for Special Learners," *T.H.E. Journal* (June):6–14.

GULLEY, D. AND F. A. SCOTT. 1989. "Lottery Effects on Pari-Mutuel Tax Revenues," *National Tax Journal,* 42(1):89–93.

HALLBERG, D. 1987. "Educators Voice Disappointment with Lottery," *Oakland California Tribune* (August 30).

HANCOCK, D. L., ed. 1987. *Handbook of U.S. Lottery Fundamentals, 1st Edition.* Washington, DC: Public Gaming Research Institute.

HARLOW, R. L. 1968. "Sharkansky and State Expenditures: A Comment," *National Tax Journal,* 21:215–216.

HARTWIG, E. 1987. *Do Our Schools Win Too? School Uses of Lottery Revenues: Year One.* Policy Paper No. PP-87-4-7. Berkeley, CA: University of California, Policy Analysis for California Education.

HEAVEY, J. F. 1978. "The Incidence of State Lottery Taxes," *Public Finance Quarterly,* 6:415.

HICKROD, G. A. 1971. "Local Demand for Education: A Critique of School Finance and Economic Research circa 1959–1969," *Review of Educational Research,* 41:35–50.

HICKROD, G. A., E. R. HINDS, G. P. ANTHONY, J. A. DIVELY AND G. B. PRUYNE. 1992. "The Effect of Constitutional Litigation on Education Finance: A Preliminary Analysis," *Journal of Education Finance,* pp. 180–210.

HILSOP, C. 1971. *Eliphalet Nott.* Middletown, CT: Wesleyan University Press.

HIRSCH, W. Z. 1960. "Determinants of Public Education Expenditures," *National Tax Journal,* 13:29–40.

HOFFERBERT, R. I. 1968. "Socioeconomic Dimensions of the American States: 1890–1960," *Midwest Journal of Political Science,* 12:401–418.

HYBELS, J. H. 1979. "The Impact of Legalization on Illegal Gambling Participation," *Journal of Social Issues,* 35(3):27–35.

ILLINOIS STATE LOTTERY. 1988. *Annual Report 1987.* Chicago, IL.

IOWA STATE LOTTERY. 1988. *Annual Report 1987.* Des Moines, IA.

JAMES, H. T., J. A. KELLY, AND W. I. GARMS. 1966. *Determinants of Educational Expenditures in Large Cities of the United States.* Stanford, CA: Stanford University, School of Education.

JANDA, K. 1990. "Videopaths to Learning American Government," in *The MacIntosh Supplement to T.H.E. Journal,* pp. 42–47.

JEWELL, R. W. "Household Demand for Public Education," unpublished doctoral dissertation, University of Chicago, 1969.

JOHNS, R. L. AND R. B. Kimbrough. 1968. *The Relationship of Socioeconomic Factors Educational Leadership Patterns,* and *Elements of Community Power.* Washington, DC: Office of Education, Bureau of Research.

JOHNS, R. L., E. L. MORPHET, AND K. ALEXANDER. 1983. *The Economics and Financing of Education.* Englewood Cliffs, NJ: Prentice-Hall.

JONES, T. H. 1985. *Introduction to School Finance: Technique and Social Policy.* New York NY: Macmillan.

JONES, T. H. Private communication with John Meskill, Chief Attorney, Connecticut Lottery Agency, October 28, 1992.

KABAK, I. W. AND J. S. SIMONOFF. 1983. "A Look at Daily Lotteries," *American Statistician,* 37:49–52.

KAHN, T. AND D. MASTER. 1992. "Multimedia Literacy at Rowland: A Good Story, Well Told," *T.H.E. Journal* (February):77–83.

KALLICK, M., D. SUITS, T. DIELMAN, AND J. HYBELS. 1977. "A Survey of American Gambling Attitudes and Behavior," Appendix 2 to *Gambling in America.* Stock No. 052-003-00254-0. Washington, DC: U.S. Government Printing Office.

KANTZER, K. S. 1983. "Gambling Everyone's a Loser," *Christianity Today,* 27(November 25):12–13.

KAPLAN, H. R. 1984. "The Social and Economic Impact of State Lotteries," *The Annals of the American Academy of Political and Social Science,* 474:91–106.

KARCHER, A. J. 1989. *Lotteries.* New Brunswick, NJ: Transaction Publishers, p. 94.

KELLERMAN, D. AND H. WULF. 1991. "State Aid to Local Governments," in *The Book of the States, Vol. 28, 1990–1991.* Lexington, KY: National Council of State Governments, pp. 549–564.

KERLINGER, F. N. 1986. *Foundations of Behavioral Research, 3rd Edition.* New York, NY: Holt, Rinehart and Winston.

KNAPP, E. S. 1988. "Lotteries No Gamble," *State Government News* (March):14.

KOZA, J. P. 1982. "Comparative Demographics of Six Types of Lottery Products," *Public Gaming* (June):22–24.

KOZA, J. P. 1987. "The Myth of the Poor Buying Lottery Tickets," in *Handbook of U.S. Lottery Fundamentals, 1st Edition,* D. L. Hancock, ed., Washington, DC: Public Gaming Research Institute, pp. 25–31.

KOZOL, J. 1991. *Savage Inequalities.* New York, NY: Crown Publishers.

KURNOW, E. 1963. "Determinants of State and Local Expenditure Reexamined," *National Tax Journal,* 16(3):252–255.

LaFLEUR, T. 1988a. "1988 Lottery Efficiency Study," *Gaming and Wagering Business* (September):18–29.

LaFleur, T. 1988b. "World Lottery Sales—$45B," *Gaming and Wagering Business* (October):1.

Landocoeur, R. and C. Mireault. 1988. "Gambling Behaviors among High School Students in the Quebec Area," *Journal of Gambling Behavior,* 4(1):3–12.

Lescault, P. R. 1983. "The Relationship among Reform, the Variance of the Distribution and the Magnitude of State Aid," *Dissertation Abstracts International,* 44:937A.

Lieberman, M. 1990. *Public School Choice: Current Issues/Future Prospects.* Lancaster, PA: Technomic Publishing Co., Inc.

Lockard, J., P. D. Abrams, and W. A. Many. 1990. *Microcomputers for Education, 2nd Edition.* Glenview, IL: Scott Foresman/Little, Brown Higher Education.

Lodge, A. 1986. "Annals of Taxation: 'A Tax on Imbeciles,' " *Journal of Accountancy,* 161:36.

MacManus, S. A. 1989. "State Lotteries Aren't a Windfall for Education," *Wall Street Journal,* 14(February 1):14.

MacManus, S. A. 1990. "Financing Federal, State and Local Governments," *Annals of the American Academy of Social and Political Sciences,* 509:22–35.

Maine State Lottery. 1988. *Annual Report 1987.* Augusta, ME.

Marshall, E. 1978. "State Lootery," *The New Republic* (June 24):20–21.

Maryland State Lottery. 1988. *Annual Report 1987.* Baltimore, MD.

Massachusetts State Lottery Commission. 1987. *Annual Report 1987.* Braintree, MA.

McCann, M. 1987. "The New Hampshire Sweepstakes Commission: The Lottery Pioneer," in *Handbook of U.S. Lottery Fundamentals,* D. L. Hancock, ed., Washington, DC: Public Gaming Research Institute, pp. 8–10.

McConkey, C. W. and W. E. Warren. 1987. "Psychographic and Demographic Profiles of State Lottery Ticket Purchasers," *Journal of Consumer Affairs,* 21:314–327.

McMahon, W. W. 1970. "An Economic Analysis of Major Determinants of Expenditures of Public Education," *Review of Economics and Statistics,* 52:242–253.

Merina, A. 1992. "New Wave: A World of Understanding," *NEA Today* (May):29.

Mikesell, J. L. and M. A. Pirog-Good. 1990. "State Lotteries and Crime," *American Journal of Economics and Sociology,* 49(1):7–19.

Mikesell, J. L. and C. K. Zorn. 1986. "State Lotteries as Fiscal Savior or Fiscal Fraud: A Look at the Evidence," *Public Administration Review,* 46:311–320.

Mikesell, J. L. and C. K. Zorn. 1987. "State Lottery Sales—Separating the Influence of Markets and Game Structure," *Growth and Change,* 18(4):10–19.

Milyo, J. D. 1986. "The Tax Incidence of the Connecticut State Lottery," unpublished master's thesis, The University of Connecticut, Storrs, CT.

Miner, J. 1963. *Social and Economic Factors in Spending for Public Education.* Syracuse, NY: Syracuse University.

Missouri State Lottery. 1987. *Annual Report 1986.* Jefferson City, MO.

Morain, D. 1987. "Lotteries on a Role Nationwide," *Los Angeles Times* (February 1).

Morehouse, S. 1981. *State Politics, Parties, and Policy.* New York, NY: Holt, Rhinehart and Winston.

Morss, E. 1966. "Some Thoughts on the Determinants of State and Local Expenditures," *National Tax Journal,* 19:95–103.

MUELLER, H. M., ed. 1935. *The Reference Shelf: Lotteries, Vol. 1.* New York, NY: H. W. Wilson.

MURPHY, J., ed. 1990. *The Educational Reform Movement of the 1980s.* Berkeley, CA: McCutchan.

THE NATIONAL CENTER FOR EFFECTIVE SCHOOLS. 1993. *National Standards, Focus in Change, No. 11.* Madison, WI: The National Center for Effective Schools, School of Education, University of Wisconsin.

NATIONAL EDUCATION ASSOCIATION. 1988a. *Estimates of School Statistics 1987–1988.* Washington, DC: National Education Association.

NATIONAL EDUCATION ASSOCIATION. 1988b. *Rankings of the States 1987.* Washington, DC: National Education Association.

NATIONAL EDUCATION ASSOCIATION. 1989. *Rankings of the States 1988.* Washington, DC: National Education Association.

NETZER, D. 1971. "When States Turn to Lotteries to Hold Down Taxes," *U.S. News and World Report* (May 24):37.

NEVIN, V. 1984. "Lotteries for Education in New York State, from Eliphalet Nott to Mario Cuomo," unpublished paper, State University of New York, Albany, NY.

NEW HAMPSHIRE SWEEPSTAKES COMMISSION. 1988. *Annual Report 1987.* Concord, NH.

NEW JERSEY LOTTERY. 1988. *Annual Report 1987.* Trenton, NJ.

NEW YORK STATE LOTTERY. 1988. *Annual Report 1987.* Albany, NY.

NUNNALLY, J. C. 1978. *Psychometric Theory, 2nd Edition.* New York, NY: McGraw-Hill.

ODDEN, A. R., ed. 1991. *Educational Policy Implementation.* Albany, NY: State University of New York Press.

OHIO STATE LOTTERY. 1988. *Annual Report 1987.* Cleveland, OH.

OHLS, J. C. AND T. J. WALES. 1972. "Supply and Demand for State and Local Services," *Review of Economics and Statistics,* 54:424–430.

OLSON, L. 1992. "Profiles in Technology: Introduction," *Teachers Magazine* (January):17–18.

OREGON STATE LOTTERY. 1988. *Annual Report 1987.* Salem, OR.

PENNSYLVANIA STATE LOTTERY. 1988. *Annual Report 1987.* Middletown, PA.

PHALON, R. 1984. "The Crying of Lot 84," *Forbes* (January 16):6–7.

PIDOT, G. B. 1969. "A Principal Components Analysis of the Determinants of Local Government Fiscal Patterns," *Review of Economics and Statistics,* 51:176–188.

PIPHO, C. 1987. "The Lottery Luster," *Phi Delta Kappan,* 69:254–255.

PIPHO, C. 1989. "Education and the State Budget Squeeze," *Phi Delta Kappan,* 70:582–583.

POGUE, T. F. AND L. G. SGONTZ. 1968. "Factors Influencing State-Local Spending: An Extension of Recent Empirical Investigations," *Mississippi Valley Journal of Business and Economics* (Fall):72–82.

POLITZER, R., J. S. MORROW, AND S. B. LEAVEY. 1982. "Report on the Societal Cost of Pathological Gambling and the Cost/Benefit Effectiveness of Treatment," *The Gambling Papers: Proceedings of the Fifth National Conference on Gambling and*

Risk Taking. Reno, NV: Bureau of Business and Economic Research, University of Nevada–Reno.

PUNCKE, M. M. 1984. "Pro and Con Statements: Are State Lotteries Considered a Regressive Tax?" in *State Lotteries: An Overview*. United States Senate, Ninety-Eighth Congress.

RENSHAW, E. F. 1960. "A Note on the Expenditure Effect of State Aid to Education," *Journal of Political Economy*, 68:170–174.

RHODE ISLAND LOTTERY. 1987. *Annual Report 1986*. Cranston, RI.

ROLLINS, H. E. 1929. *The Pepys Ballads, Volume 1*. Cambridge, MA: Harvard University Press, pp. 24–31.

ROSEN, S. AND D. NORTON. 1966. "The Lottery as a Source of Public Revenue," *Taxes*, 44:617–625.

ROSENTHAL, A. 1980. "Shaping State Education Policy," *Compact*, 14:36–38.

ROSS, I. 1984. "Corporate Winners in the Lottery Boom," *Fortune* (September 3):20–25.

ROSSMILLER, R. A. 1968. "Consensus, Conflict, and Expenditures for Education," *Proceedings of the Eleventh National Conference on School Finance of the National Education Association*.

RYAN, J. E. 1985. "State and Local Expenditures for Public Education: A Simultaneous Equation Approach," *Dissertation Abstracts International*, 46:2437A.

SACKS, S. AND R. HARRIS. 1964. "The Determinants of State and Local Government Expenditures and Intergovernmental Flows of Funds," *National Tax Journal*, 17:75–85.

SACKS, S. AND W. F. HELLMUTH, JR. 1961. *Financing Government in a Metropolitan Government*. Glencoe, IL: Free Press.

SACKS, S. AND D. C. RANNEY. 1967. "Suburban Education: A Fiscal Analysis," in *Educating an Urban Population*, M. Gittell, ed., Beverly Hills, CA: Sage Publications.

SAMPLE, H. A. 1987. "Fast-Growing Lottery Catches its Breath at 2," *Sacramento Bee* (September 3).

SAMUELSON, P. A. 1958. "Aspects of Public Expenditure Theories," *Review of Economics and Statistics*, 40:332–338.

SARASOHN, D. 1983. "The Bookie State," *New Republic* (February 7):11–13.

SCHNEIDER, J. 1987. "Is It Worth It?" *Lansing State Journal* (April 5).

SCHULTZE, S. 1987. "Would a State Lottery Take Toll on the Poor?" *Milwaukee Journal* (March 22).

SERGI, T. S. 1977. "The Relationship between Socio-Economic, Demographic, and Municipal Characteristics of Connecticut School Districts and Their Local Demand for Education," *Dissertation Abstracts International*, 38:4496A.

SHAPIRO, J. P. 1988. "The Dark Side of America's Lotto-Mania," *U.S. News and World Report* (September 19):21, 24.

SHAPIRO, S. 1962. "Some Socio-Economic Determinants of Expenditures for Education," *Comparative Education Review*, 6:160–166.

SHARKANSKY, I. 1967. "Regional Patterns of Expenditures of American States," *Western Political Science Quarterly*, 20:955–971.

SHARKANSKY, I. 1968. "A Reply to Professor Harlow," *National Tax Journal,* 21:217–219.

SHIPPEE, G. E., D. J. SCHWARTZMAN AND K. REYNOLDS. 1983. "Using Demographics to Increase Lottery Sales," *Public Gaming* (August).

SHOSTECK, H. S. 1967. *The Socioeconomic Conditions for Support of Public Education.* Madison, WI: University of Wisconsin.

SIRKIN, J. R. 1985. "Lotteries: 'Mega-Bucks' Promise Is Disputed," *Education Week* (September 18):1, 13–14.

SMITH, J. F. AND V. ABT. 1984. "Gambling as Play," *The Annals of the American Academy of Political and Social Science,* 474:122–132.

SNIDER, W. 1987. "Lotteries' Promises Clouded by Problems in Number of States," *Education Week* (March 4):1, 22.

SPARKMAN, W. E. 1977. "The Relationship between Socioeconomic Variables and State Effort for Education," *Journal of Education Finance,* 2:335–355.

STARK, S. D., D. S. HONEYMAN, AND R. C. WOOD. 1991. *An Examination of the Florida Education Lottery.* Occasional Paper No. 3. Gainesville, FL: UCEA Center for Education Finance, Department of Educational Leadership, University of Florida.

STEWART, M. J. 1987. "Patterns of Revenues for Public Elementary and Secondary School Education Derived as a Result of State Lotteries: A Case Study of Michigan and New York," *Dissertation Abstracts International,* 48:1114A.

STOCKER, F. D. 1972. "State Sponsored Gambling as a Source of Public Revenue," *National Tax Journal,* 25:437–441.

STOKEY, E. AND R. ZECKHAUSER. 1978. *A Primer for Policy Analysis.* New York, NY: W. W. Norton & Company.

STOVER, M. E. 1987. "Revenue Potential of State Lotteries," *Public Finance Quarterly,* 15:428–440.

STOVER, M. E. 1990. "Contiguous State Lotteries—Substitutes or Complement," *Journal of Policy Analysis and Management,* 9(4):565–568.

STRUDWICK, J. A. 1985. "An Analysis of Spatial and Social Inequalities in Educational Finance: United States and Great Britain, 1870–1970," doctoral dissertation, University of Toronto, 1984, *Dissertation Abstracts International,* 46:1189A.

SUITS, D. B. 1977. "Gambling Taxes: Regressivity and Revenue Potential," *National Tax Journal,* 30(1):19–36.

SUITS, D. B. 1979. "Economic Background for Gambling Policy," *Journal of Social Issues,* 59.

SULLIVAN, G. 1972. *By Chance a Winner: The History of Lotteries.* New York, NY: Mead.

TABACHNICK, B. G. AND L. S. FIDELL. 1983. *Using Multivariate Statistics.* New York, NY: Harper & Row.

TAX FOUNDATION. 1965. *Earmarked State Taxes.* Research Publication No. 2. New York, NY: Tax Foundation.

THOMAS, S. B. AND L. D. WEBB. 1984. "The Use and Abuse of Lotteries as a Revenue Source," *Journal of Education Finance,* 9:289–311.

TIFFT, S. 1984. "Gambling on a Way to Trim Taxes," *Time* (May 28):42.

TUFTE, E. R. 1974. *Data Analysis for Politics and Policy.* Englewood Cliffs, NJ: Prentice-Hall.

U.S. BUREAU OF THE CENSUS. 1982. *Statistical Abstract of the U.S.: 1982–1983, 103rd Edition.* Washington, DC: U.S. Government Printing Office.

U.S. BUREAU OF THE CENSUS. 1986. *State and Metropolitan Area Data Book: 1986.* Washington, DC: U.S. Government Printing Office.

U.S. BUREAU OF THE CENSUS. 1987. *Statistical Abstract of the U.S.: 1988, 108th Edition.* Washington, DC: U.S. Government Printing Office.

U.S. BUREAU OF THE CENSUS. 1988a. *Government Finances in 1986–1987.* Washington, DC: U.S. Government Printing Office.

U.S. BUREAU OF THE CENSUS. 1988b. *State Government Finances in 1987.* Washington, DC: U.S. Government Printing Office.

U.S. CONGRESS. 1988. Charity Games Advertising Clarification Act of 1988, 18 LISC 1301, Public Law 100-625, Nov. 7, 1988.

U.S. CONGRESS, SENATE COMMITTEE ON GOVERNMENTAL AFFAIRS. 1984. *State Lotteries: An Overview.* Hearing Before the Subcommittee on Intergovernmental Relations, Ninety-Eighth Congress.

U.S. DEPARTMENT OF EDUCATION, NATIONAL CENTER FOR EDUCATIONAL STATISTICS. 1987. *Digest of School Statistics: 1987.* Washington, DC: U.S. Government Printing Office.

U.S. DEPARTMENT OF EDUCATION, NATIONAL CENTER FOR EDUCATIONAL STATISTICS. 1988. *Common Core of Data.* Washington, DC: U.S. Government Printing Office.

VACHE, J. D. 1990. "The Net Revenue Effect of California's Lottery," *Journal of Policy Analysis and Management,* 9(4):561–564.

VAN DE KAMP, J. K. 1984. "Lotteries: More Minuses than Pluses," *Sacramento Union* (March 8):4–5.

VANCE, J. 1989. *An Analysis of the Costs and Benefits of Lotteries: The Canadian Experience.* Lewiston, NY: E. Mellen Publishing Co.

VANCE, J. 1986. "Canadian State Lotteries: 1970–1984," Ph.D. thesis, Carleton University, Ottawa, Canada.

VERMONT LOTTERY COMMISSION. 1988. *Annual Report 1987.* South Barre, VT.

VON DREHLE, D. 1987. "Will Lottery Help Schools? Don't Bet on It, Critics Say," *Miami Herald* (January 7).

VROOMAN, D. H. 1976. "An Economic Analysis of the New York State Lottery," *National Tax Journal,* 29:482–489.

WALL, J. M. 1990. "Unbinding the Devil in Georgia," *The Christian Century,* 107(November 21):1083.

WASHINGTON STATE LOTTERY. 1988. *Annual Report 1987.* Olympia, WA.

WEINSTEIN, D. AND L. DEITCH. 1974. *The Impact of Legalized Gambling: The Socioeconomic Consequences of Lotteries and Off-Track Betting,* New York, NY: Praeger.

WENTZLER, N. 1980. "Wealth Neutrality and the Demand for Education," *National Tax Journal,* 33:237–238.

WEST VIRGINIA LOTTERY. 1988. *Annual Report 1987.* Charleston, WV.

WILL, G. F. 1989. "In the Grip of Gambling," *Newsweek* (May 8):78.

WU, R. Y. 1979. "A Cross-Section Study on the Demand for State Lottery Tickets," *American Economist,* 23:6–11.

YOSHIHASHI, P. 1991. "Disney Bets on Lottery Show to Hit Jackpot," *The Wall Street Journal* (April 5):81.

ZEIGLER, H. AND K. JOHNSON. 1972. *The Politics of Education in the States.* New York, NY: Bobbs-Merrill.

INDEX

187